FOURTH WAY TEACHINGS

Practical Methods on Inner Transformation

by

Rebecca Nottingham

Published by

Theosis Books

www.theosisbooks.com

© 2010 by Rebecca Nottingham

ISBN 0-9664960-4-3

Printed in the United States of America.

Table of Contents

PART I   WRITINGS

PART II   TEACHINGS

INTRODUCTION

The Work is a system of psychological practices and ideas designed to increase Consciousness in a human being. It teaches that humans exist in a state called Sleep which is a level of Consciousness characterized by an automatic stimulus-response nature arising from self-love.

Understand, from the beginning, that the Work is a definite process with a specific aim. The Aim of the Work I's to develop or raise your level of Consciousness. Consciousness is reflected in Being, therefore Being must evolve along with Consciousness. They are not separable. Being is Goodness and manifests Conscience.

Everyone has conscience and it will grow in proportion to Consciousness, as well. Goodness reflects Conscience to the exact extent of its development.

So understand that the ultimate aim of the process of the Work is to create authentic goodness in a person. A stable, unified Conscious Being who can act from self-transcendent goodness instead of self-love.

The process of doing the Work begins with sincere desire to acquire the Knowledge of ideas and practices. It can only begin to create a transformation within you when you begin to apply the practices and ideas to yourself. Knowing about it, thinking about it, talking about it will not lead to change. Change requires internal effort and only the student can supply the force of effort that creates change. In the case of this Work, change means transformation from Sleep to awakened Consciousness from ego-centric psychology to self-transcendent psychology. The process can be described in general as the purifying of the Emotional Center. That means eliminating all of the Wrong Work of the Emotional Center which is studied in detail and from a particular angle. This angle is the perspective of uncritical Self-Observation. Self-Observation is the foundational practice in the Work and it can evolve into a permanent perspective of awareness.

Self-Observation is directed at your psychology. It provides illumination for your Work but what you see within yourself in the light of Self-Observation is shocking and usually abhorrent. It takes tenacious and repeated efforts to practice Self-Observation correctly, that is, with enough Objectivity to be uncritical about what you observe, and enough Conscience to not want to have to observe any particular Wrong Work again.

The light of Self-Observation will begin a change within your psychology as you see yourself in the light of Objective Truth.

It is only when you get to this point, after having learned, and practiced repeatedly, that you will know what the Work requires of you and you will have to decide at that point if you want to continue. Every bit of progress depends on your sincere effort so the continuing is always up to you. If you proceed in the Work you will feel worse before you feel better. You will observe, like a bound and gagged prisoner, while your Personality goes around acting in ways and saying things that in no way reflect what is most real in yourself -- Real I. You will sound insincere to yourself and you will feel disempowered. You will experience a feeling of psychological vertigo as you lose Acquired Personality before true Personality has had time to grow. You will come to a point, intermittently at first, when the strength of Real I can direct Personality.

Your Work Memory, which is the memory of everything that you have verified for yourself through Self-Observation, will grow and gain clarity and have force. You will find that this process of gaining something Consciousness) requires mostly losing things, the thoughts and emotions that make up the noise in your mind, primarily, so that there is a place that can receive. You will find that you have to Work your way up, through conscious effort, to a place where you can begin to receive illumination from Higher Consciousness. And what you will find is that the psychological position from which we can be receptive is characterized by

Humility. Humility has no requirements and thereby enough inner silence to enable reception.

So in the Work you are on a developmental path that, when it is successful, produces higher enlightened Consciousness which has a corresponding development in Conscience, reflected in Humility, and Being, which is Goodness.

Be sure that this is what you are seeking -- To be humble and pure in heart and at the service of Goodness. If you are seeking personal power you will not find it in worldly terms in the Work. So don't come to the Work expecting to receive great transforming experiences. You will receive tools. You will have to use them yourself to create transformation out of effort -- WORK. You will experience resistance internally and externally. You will no longer be going with the flow. You will have turned around and so the flow will be going against you.

The reason to undertake all of this Work may not seem clear but it is very simple. We do the Work in order to become more than mechanical and Asleep in the world and in doing so we find the fulfillment of the meaning of our existence in this life. As a consequence you will find peace, not necessarily in your life, but in your heart and mind.

PART I

WRITINGS

BACKGROUND

I

The reason that the history of humanity is so grotesquely violent and perverted is precisely because human beings always take these ideas of personal transformation as an external map for gaining personal power. To sense-based humanity, this is always understood as finding in external events and things, objects and places, some sort of magical or corporal power, some formulation that provided the mystical transformation from mortal to immortal.

In the existing mystical metaphors for transformation, this transformation involves sacrifice and death and rebirth. All of these "religious" and esoteric teachings are meant to be applied to the practitioner himself or herself; not to others or in an external way.

There is a process for the real transformation of a human animal into a conscious human being. It is not hidden in the secret society sense. It is an internal, psychological process and therefore unseen. Esoteric doesn't mean hidden or secret. It means inner -- the inner meaning of a thing.

Human beings always behave as they always have because their individual psychologies are based on the same drives arising from the instinctive urges in place to propagate the species.

The development (transformation) beyond the automatic, self-interested motivation for life is psychological evolution. This evolution is possible but requires intentional and specific efforts that lead to humility and goodness above all.

There is no short-cut, no external way, to develop the Being, purity of spirit, required for conscious awakening, which is the rebirth of the individual. This path of conscious evolution is the straight and narrow path the initiate must follow. It leads to goodness, new level of understanding, the freedom and joy of humility, unconditional love, forgiveness, peace, acceptance, and the realization of meaning in your life.

II

Gurdjieff's Teaching is solidly linked with early Eastern Orthodox Christianity. You will find the same ideas expressed in the Philokalia, the early Desert Fathers, and in Christian Orthodox traditional practices such as the "watch of the heart". His dismissal of students, which is notoriously rather severe and abrupt, had more to do with the fact that the students were looking for someone to worship, someone to tell them what to do and how to do it. These types of people always gather around a Teacher and any real Teacher wants their students to graduate. Those who didn't or couldn't, and those who formed worshipful attitudes toward him, he dismissed. Those who weren't serious, he dismissed.

There isn't a way to know exactly what the Work is about from outside You have to be in the Work in order to understand what it is about. So a lot of people come into the Work thinking it is one thing and then find that they are not interested in or willing to accept what it really is. Lots of those people were just put out. There is no place for non-serious students. It is a waste of the student's time, a waste of the Teacher's time.

Gurdjieff brought the expression of transformation that works. He himself called it esoteric Christianity. It contains Objective Truth. You will find Objective Truth in other places besides esoteric Christianity, but this particular system is unique because it is practical, and although it is very difficult, if an individual has the desire and makes the efforts with the right motives, real psychological change, real transformation of Consciousness is possible -- that means real psychological evolution, raising your level of Being through intentional, specific efforts

The system called the Fourth Way is presented in the world as a system that begins with the cosmology that Gurdjieff put forth. It is fascinating mind-altering experience to discover this cosmology and credit it even a little bit. But that is the exoteric aspect of the Fourth Way and it is where ninety-nine percent of all the people in the Work exist, talking about the ideas, the concepts, the cosmology, the table of hydrogens, the law of octaves, the law of Three, the law of Seven, Triads, the Ray of Creation, the cosmoses, etc.

The cosmology is unverifiable and fascinating. However, it creates no actual transformation in a human being, unless it leads them into the psychological teaching of the Work. These psychological ideas are best expressed by Maurice Nicoll, in the Commentaries. The ideas, although they are not presented in a progressive fashion or according to a syllabus, nevertheless is a whole teaching with a beginning place. And if one begins aright with practices, and with a correct understanding of the ideas, great personal change is possible; real personal transformation, to a higher level of consciousness, and a purity of heart that is exemplified in humility. These things are possible and more for a serious student who is sincere, unselfish, and puts long-term efforts into the Work. Humility in this Work means the same as "poor in spirit". And for those who have humility, who are poor in spirit, "theirs is the Kingdom of Heaven". The Kingdom of Heaven in the Work is called higher consciousness. It is accessible through the Work but not very many people are interested in acquiring humility.

BUILDING A SOUL OR BAPTISM

One of the basic ideas of the Gurdjieff teaching that has been mistaught is the idea of building a soul. This is a very foundational idea and is, I believe, a misunderstanding of the spiritual concept intended. It springs from a lower level of Understanding, one that says that man does not have a soul until he builds a soul and a man builds his soul basically by the practice of the Work. Whatever name you want to attribute to it -- the process is divinization, becoming Conscious, transcending self-interest.

In the Fourth Way cosmology, it is taught that one builds a soul that can exist in Eternity, in the electronic world, through studious efforts. But since this is esoteric Christianity, the real understanding of this idea is not that you build your own soul -- you can't create your own soul. If you could the result would be a self-created Frankenstein made from your own limitations. What you can do, through this Work, is to create a purified place within yourself where what is called the Holy Spirit in Christian terms can exist within you. This place is in Higher Consciousness. If there is no place within you that is clean enough of self-interest, then you are not accessible to higher influences and the Spirit cannot penetrate and baptize you because there is no receptive place where it can enter.

The Work is about purifying the psychology and emotions, cleaning a place within in order to be open, to be able to be receptive and hear from what the Work calls Higher Centers -- or from higher consciousness, or from what is above spiritually speaking. So the process of baptism in the Christian tradition is a reversal of the exoteric practice of submerging an individual in water. To symbolically immerse the individual in the Holy Spirit is a reversal of the real process. It is not you who enters the Holy Spirit and comes out imbued with it. The Holy Spirit enters you and only to the extent that you are open and have a place that is receptive within you. The Work makes this place. The process is painful, ego-denying, and worth it. This experience is universal and the authentic process and transformational experience is the same for all people in all times, and is RECOGNIZABLE in different forms, therefore verifiable.

Currently the largest distortion in all the mainline Gurdjieffian schools is the idea that, since you are asleep and since you are a multiplicity, that you cannot discern what is real and what is unreal either within you or in the tangible world around you. This is a deliberately cultivated miscommunication of this idea that is used by the current "schools" in order to keep students paying money to the teacher so that they can learn how to become conscious enough to know what is real in them. The reality is that Conscience can discern.

III

If you are interested in the powers you will gain through doing the Work you should know exactly what they are. You will be able to transcend your personal needs on behalf of the good of others. You will no longer feel competitive. You will not feel the need to assert yourself and you will be able to if appropriate. Your actions will be motivated by Goodness only, because Goodness is the nature of Being. Your Real I will not be tossed around by the circumstances of life. Real I will simply respond appropriately, always creating Goodness. You will suffer less, subjectively, and you will suffer more, objectively. You will not feel inclined to go along with anything except Conscience. Your Conscience will grow and assert influence that can create real permanent change -- evolution. You will experience peace, acceptance, serenity, appreciation, gratitude, joy, humility, forgiveness, freedom, conscious inspiration, intentionality in action.

You may well have heard some of these ideas from other sources in devolved forms. The potential powers offered to the student in existing Fourth Way schools are from the psychological level of sense-based thinking. They say you will gain self-mastery and the power to "do". You will awaken to the illusion of life. You will become a higher self, an improved version of yourself. You will develop your Real I. You will become free of the ordinary laws that govern people's lives and be able to act intentionally and get the results you are aiming at. You will receive knowledge not available outside of the "school". You will gain self-knowledge. You will experience higher conscious states. You will come under the direct power of C Influence. You will have understanding that sleeping humanity does not possess. You will learn esoteric secrets about how to create your soul. You will be able to create your own soul and that will give you immortality. You will become an immortal unlike others who will "die like dogs".

It is important to note that none of these expressions of powers are a lie. They are a lower level of expression of the Objective Truth behind them, consequently a distortion. They do not express the context or the aim of the Work. They are aimed at attracting Personality. Whether that distortion is intentional or a manifestation of a lack of Being isn't really the point. The point is that a person cannot grow in the Work if their motives are self-interested. It is the wrong angle of approach and has no force. So everyone coming into the Work needs to understand from the outset that it is far more about giving up self-interest and giving up gratification-seeking, than gaining personal power. Also that this giving up of self requires immeasurable efforts -- WORK.

The Work is a path to Conscious Evolution. This Teaching is not "my" Teaching. It is not even Gurdjieff's or Ouspensky's or Nicoll's Teaching. It could be said quite accurately that it is Christ's Teaching and still, with a particular understanding of Time, encompasses all Teaching of Objective Truth throughout human history. The expression it was given through Gurdjieff, Ouspensky and Nicoll, bears witness to the content.

IV

The Movements attract the Moving and Instinctive Centers and teach a particular discipline. The cosmology attracts Intellectual Center and schools it to think differently, psychologically. Both are exoteric and are meant to lead the student into the psycho-transformational ideas that can create real personal change and growth if understood and practiced correctly.

There is no existing group that is doing practical Work using the psychological ideas correctly. This very real tragedy means the loss of this particular path of esoteric Christianity which leads to the development of Consciousness and Being. Unless individuals can find their way to the truth of the Work, this door will close.

All of the outer forms of religions are subject to interpretations from Personality and lower levels of understanding. The Objective Truth, esoteric meaning, does not change although interpretation and level of Understanding renders it obscure. Objective Truth exists in other forms and traditions, and always has. However, the Work is the purest expression of Objective Truth. Its Aim is to teach Understanding of Objective Truth through practical experience. The psychological ideas are specifically directed so that the practitioners can verify for themselves the Objective Truth at the heart of this Teaching. That practical and verified experience creates organic Understanding which transforms Consciousness and Being. This process depends almost entirely on the personal efforts each person makes. Knowledge and guidance from verified Understanding is also necessary. Extremely few individuals can traverse the Path of the Work without guidance which is about understanding the Teaching, not about obedience to the Teacher. No intelligent person sincerely involved in the Work would reject Understanding. And since the Work says that you must verify everything for yourself through experiential Understanding, you need not take your Teacher's word on anything. You need only to understand and apply the psychological ideas to yourself to verify their objective Truth. Then you will have Understanding which can change Being.

All of the Work is to raise your level of Consciousness and evolve your Being. It is personal, interior psychological Work because that is where development can happen. Your Being which is a manifestation of Consciousness is an expression of your psychology. The aim of the process is to deconstruct the Acquired Personality, the ego, by way of efforts that illuminate and disempower it. The objective here is to purify the psychology of what is false and inauthentic and self-interested and negative because these psychological conditions obstruct the development of Consciousness. These elements are studied, addressed, and transcended leaving a more purified heart and mind, Emotional Center and Intellectual Center, feelings and thoughts, i.e. PSYCHOLOGY, that can be receptive to the Objective Truth of spiritual Being. This Work, which begins with Know Thyself, is called self-evolution because it is only through sincere efforts intentionally made by yourself, that the possibility of evolution exists. It is in and through the energy of the effort that evolution happens. Each person must make their own efforts -- Work -- in order to evolve. No one can evolve by absorbing something, by vicinity, by osmosis, by knowledge. Only personal Work effort produces evolution.

The Work is difficult in places, it is dangerous in places, and it is painful often enough. The results, however, are liberating. This process of the Work, of becoming your Real I, deconstructing Acquired Personality whose substance is self-interest, leads to Humility which is liberating. To be without gratification requirements, i.e. detachment, i.e. Non-Identified, leaves you free and open to inspiration, receptive and available for service.

V

I began with the intention of answering questions about the Work within the context of its Aim. This point of view seems to have been left out of the repudiated surviving Gurdjieff "schools". Mostly by intention.

In any Teaching, including legitimate paths to self-transcendence, the external forms that a particular one takes after the demise of the Teacher, are always from a lower level of Understanding and Being. Though they may carry the Teaching, as a vessel carries cargo, it is the vessel that is seen in the world. What is inside remains esoteric even to the crew of the vessel. These forms most commonly represent the lowest common denominator in Understanding. That makes them literal and formatory and fixed. And that leaves them without the "spirit" of the Teaching apparent in its worldly form. This common denominator often includes worship of the Teacher which no legitimate Teacher ever wants or asks for. It is always, however, an easy way for the student to stay on the surface of the Teaching without entering into the path.

Some forms represent the perversions or distortions or level of Being of their various leaders unintentionally. Some forms remain rigidly crystallized in formatory dogma to assure absolute adherence to the original teacher's literal words and therefore insure and validate its members own understanding of the Teaching. Some forms have been created that deliberately misuse the ideas and misrepresent the Teaching for the purpose of personal gain for the Teacher.

This is and always has been the way every religious path degenerates after the Teacher has gone. This is so because from that point on the Teaching is conveyed to the world through the level of Being and Understanding of the conveyor. This includes the crystallization of the spirit of the Teaching into words, formulations, rituals and physical exercises, and teacher worship. It also includes criminal intentionality since that belongs to the nature of human beings as well.

With no instruction at all, anyone can find clear examples of these forms in the Fourth Way schools and organizations and groups existing today. What is always tragic is that the forms themselves serve to prevent the student from entering the path since they satisfy and entrap the lowest common denominator. What is always possible, however, is that something higher in the student will lead them to find the cargo, the spirit, the inner meaning, and the Aim of the Teaching, the esoteric understanding of the ideas in the Teaching -- those that have the power of transformation.

In the Gurdjieff tradition, the Fourth Way, the esoteric teaching is called the Work. The ideas belonging to this esoteric level are about personal, psychological evolution and they require real personal efforts to create experiential Understanding. You may take the Gurdjieffian cosmology or leave it, but no one can advance in the Work, gain in evolution of Consciousness and Being, without practicing and applying the psycho-transformational ideas to themselves with sincerity and tenacity. If the ideas are understood rightly and practiced in earnest, the results are true spiritual growth, the development of Consciousness and Being. Since that is the authentic potential of the path called the Work, the tragic consequences of its existing external forms are monumental. These currently existing "schools" or groups or organizations sell the Fourth Way, literally, by promising the student (customer) a literal step-by-step system through which they will gain personal power, expanded consciousness, self-realization, freedom from natural laws, superiority over others, even immortality. These subtle distortions, intentional or otherwise, represent not only the limitation of Understanding and Being at the source, but more importantly they misrepresent the Aim of the Work. Since the Work is esoteric Christianity, these kinds of gains are impossible because they are antithetical to esoteric Christian teaching.

The Work, which is called esoteric Christianity by Gurdjieff, Ouspensky and Nicoll, is not given in context in any successful school in the world. That is because it doesn't sell well when offered as a path to Humility. But by selling the Work as a formulation or path to personal power, many are attracted and most are easily satisfied by paying money to receive supposedly secret knowledge that will transform them and bestow the aforementioned powers. In this, the distortion of the metaphysical idea of payment is used to filch the student.

What dimension and depth of criminality this rape of the Work expresses. And how tragic the loss of real spiritual potential.

FOURTH WAY GROUP WORK

Esoteric does not mean hidden in a secret way. It refers to the inner meaning of a Teaching and is accessible to any ardent, earnest seeker.

Gurdjieff called the Work esoteric Christianity. Objective Truth makes it universally applicable. This particular system of transformation is unique because it is practical and real psychological change, real transformation of consciousness is possible -- that means, real psychological evolution, raising your level of Being through intentional, specific efforts. The Work is called the Work because it requires great efforts. These efforts are almost entirely internal, psychological. The system called the Fourth Way is presented in the world as a system that begins with the cosmology that Gurdjieff put forth. It is fascinating mind-altering experience to discover this cosmology and credit it even a little bit. But that is the exoteric aspect of the Fourth Way and it is where ninety-nine percent of all the people in the Work exist, talking about the ideas, the concepts, the cosmology, the table of hydrogens, the law of octaves, the law of Three, the law of Seven, Triads, the Ray of Creation, the cosmoses, etc.

The cosmology is fascinating. However, it creates no actual transformation in a human being, unless it leads them into the psychological teaching of the Work. These psychological ideas are best expressed by Maurice Nicoll, in his "Psychological Commentaries on the Teachings of Gurdjieff and Ouspensky", particularly. The ideas have a beginning place and progression, and if one begins aright with practices, and with a correct understanding of the ideas, great personal change is possible -- real personal transformation to a higher level of consciousness, a purity of
heart that is exemplified in humility. This experience is universal and the authentic process and transformational experience is the same for all people in all times and is recognizable, therefore verifiable.

If you are interested in the powers you will gain through doing the Work you should know exactly what they are. You will be able to transcend your personal needs on behalf of the good of others. You will no longer feel competitive or that you have to "prove" yourself. You will not feel the need to assert yourself and you will be able to do so, if appropriate. Your actions will be motivated by Goodness only, because Goodness is the nature of Being. Your Real I will not be
emotionally tossed around by the circumstances of life. Real I will

simply respond appropriately, always creating Goodness. You will suffer less, subjectively, and you will suffer more, objectively. You will not feel inclined to go along with anything except Conscience. Your Conscience will grow and assert influence that can create real permanent change -- psychological evolution. You will experience peace, acceptance, serenity, appreciation, gratitude, joy, humility, forgiveness, freedom, conscious inspiration, intentionality in action.

You may well have heard some of these ideas from other sources in devolved forms. The potential powers offered to the student in existing Fourth Way schools and other "New Age"developmental paths are from the psychological level of sense-based thinking. They say you will gain self-mastery and the power to "do". You will awaken to the illusion of life. You will become a higher self, an improved, empowered version of yourself. You will develop your Real Self. You will become free of the ordinary laws that govern other people's lives and be able to act purposefully to get the results you are aiming at. You will receive knowledge not available outside of the "school". You will gain self-knowledge. You will experience higher conscious states. You will come under the direct power of C Influence. You will have understanding that sleeping humanity does not possess. You will learn esoteric secrets about how to create your soul. You will be able to create your own soul and that will give you immortality. You will belong to a privileged, elite community.

It is important to note that none of these expressions of powers are a lie. They are a lower level of expression of the Objective Truth behind them, consequently a distortion. They do not express the context or the aim of the Work. They are aimed at attracting Personality. Whether that distortion is intentional or a manifestation of a lack of Being isn't really the point. The point is that a person cannot grow in the Work if their motives are self-interested. It is the wrong angle of approach and has no force. So everyone coming into the Work needs to understand from the outset that it is far more about giving up self-interest and giving up gratification-seeking, than gaining personal power. Also that this giving up of self requires immeasurable efforts -- WORK.

The Work is a path to Conscious Evolution. This Teaching is not "my" Teaching. It is not even Gurdjieff's or Ouspensky's or Nicoll's Teaching. It could be said quite accurately that it is Christ's Teaching, and with a particular understanding of Time, encompasses all Teaching of Objective Truth throughout human history. The expression it was given through Gurdjieff, Ouspensky and Nicoll, bears witness to the content.

All of the Work is to raise your level of Consciousness and evolve your Being. It is personal, interior psychological Work because that is where development can happen. Your level of Being which is an expression of your psychology. The aim of the Work process is to deconstruct the Acquired Personality, the ego, by way of efforts that illuminate and disempower it. The objective here is to purify the psychology of what is false and inauthentic and self-interested and negative because these psychological conditions obstruct the development of Consciousness. These elements are studied, addressed, and transcended leaving a more purified heart and mind, Emotional Center and Intellectual Center, feelings and thoughts, i.e. PSYCHOLOGY. This condition can be receptive to the Objective Truth of spiritual enlightenment. This Work, which begins with Know Thyself, is called self-evolution because it is only through sincere efforts intentionally made by yourself, that the possibility of evolution exists. It is in and through the energy of the effort that evolution happens. Each person must make their own efforts -- Work -- in order to evolve. No one can evolve by believing something, by vicinity, by osmosis, or by knowledge. Only personal Work effort produces evolution.

The Work is difficult in places, it is dangerous in places, and it is painful often enough. The results, however, are liberating. This process of the Work, of becoming your Real I leads to Humility which is liberating. To be without gratification requirements, i.e. detachment, i.e. Non-Identified, leaves you free and receptive and open to inspiration from Above.

All of this means to awaken from Sleep.

We do this to become the unique vessel we were created to be in order to express creation, the nature of God, in our own existence, in this life, in this world. In doing so, we become perfect servants of Goodness and find the fulfillment of meaning in our personal existence.

THE PSYCHOLOGICAL WORK OF THE FOURTH WAY

The Work is fundamentally different from other paths to conscious development in a few very important ways. To begin with, although it is a psychological system, the Work differs from standard psychology's presupposition that a human being has consciousness. Modern psychology presumes that a person who is awake and walking around has consciousness, however deformed. The Work asserts that every person in this "waking state" is in reality in a state of Waking Sleep, and that there is very little consciousness present. But it also teaches that consciousness can be developed through specific intentional efforts.

The Work teaches how to develop your consciousness through ideas and psychological practices that build new Understanding. It creates a pure heart and a self-transcendent Being which are open to illumination, perception, Understanding, and the inspiration from higher Mind, Consciousness that belongs to the spiritual level. As wonderful as this sounds, it requires a great inner struggle against the assertions of Personality and against the momentum of being Asleep in life.

Gurdjieff, Ouspensky, and Nicoll all called it esoteric Christianity so there is no reason to discard this context. If you understand that the esoteric teaching in Christianity is a teaching about Objective Truth then you can understand that all teaching about Objective Truth can be the same path from the same source throughout human history expressed in cultural and historical terms. Using Christian teaching on the idea of self-transformation gives the Work a solid philosophical and ethical grounding that has been left out of the successful Gurdjieff schools or groups. The Objective

Truth contained in this Teaching can be verified through personal experience. One of the unique aspects of this Work is that it can also be verified without religious designation because Objective Truth is the same everywhere all of the time for everyone.

The next idea is one that is essential in the direction of the Work. It differs from every religious tradition and humanity's general presupposition that God's will is done on earth.. God's will is not done on earth and this is verifiable. All of the evil and suffering that you see in the world are not the results of God's will, for God's nature is ONE. That one characteristic is Perfect Goodness; it is the will of individuals acting and living out of self-interested motivations that creates the chaos of violence . The will of God is not done on earth. The will of man is done on earth.

Nicoll: "...Religious people usually imagine that what happens on earth is always God's will, and they seek to comfort and strengthen one another with this thought, even in the face of the most senseless and fortuitous accidents, disaster and death. People who are not religious take it as evidence that there is no God...People judge of the existence or non-existence of God from what happens on earth. Every decade books are written proving that the existence of God is impossible in view of the fact that there is so much evil in life, and so much cruelty and waste in nature, while most people in the privacy of their own thoughts come to a similar conclusion. In the face of this, and arguing from the standpoint of the visible world, is it possible to believe that God -- as the supreme principle of highest Good -- exists?...If we always look to visible life for evidence of the existence or non-existence of God nothing will come of it. Therefore, to draw conclusions about God from what happens on earth is to start from an entirely wrong point of view. People continually start from this wrong level...They regard the visible external world as the first theater of divine vengeance and see in its events the hand of God punishing or rewarding human beings according to their behavior. They see God as right or justice on earth. They see the hand of God in war and believe that God is on their side and that victory will mean that the will of God is fulfilled. It is this external, sense-based idea of religion that is rebuked by Christ. He says that all people suffer the same fate unless they repent, but what is to *repent*?

"The word translated throughout the New Testament as "repentance" is in the Greek "meta-noia" which means change of mind. The Greek particle "meta" is found in several words of comparatively ordinary usage, such as metaphor, metaphysics, metamorphosis. Let us take metaphor; it means transference of meaning. To speak metaphorically is to speak beyond the literal words, to carry over or beyond and so transfer the meaning of what is said beyond the words used. Metaphysics, again, refers to the study of what is beyond purely observable physical science, such as the study of the nature of being or the theory of knowledge or the fact of consciousness. Metamorphosis is used to describe the transformation of form in insect life, the transformation of a grub into a butterfly -- a transference or transformation of structure into an entirely new structure, into something beyond. The particle "meta" therefore indicates transference, or transformation, or beyondness. The other part of this word translated as repentance -- noia -- is from the Greek words "nous" which means mind. The word metanoia has to do with the transformation of the mind in its essential meaning."

So the Work is a Teaching about the process called Metanoia which is a psychological reorientation.

Nicoll: "Here lies one of the deepest ideas in the psychological teachings of the Gospels. A radical, permanent transformation is taught as being possible and Metanoia is the technical description of it. But a man cannot reach a permanent higher level of himself unless there is built up in him a connection of ideas that can gradually lift him beyond his present level. The idea of the self-evolution of Man, the idea of Metanoia or transformation of mind, and the idea of the Kingdom of Heaven are all connected and related ideas...Christ's teaching is about a possible individual evolution in a man...Everyone on this planet is capable of a certain inner growth and individual development, and this is his true significance and his deepest meaning, and begins with Metanoia.....If we wish to begin to understand the technical meaning of the teaching in the Gospels it is necessary to get rid of all sentimental views about its import. The inner meaning of Christ's teaching is not sentimental. It has nothing to do with comforting weak and useless people or encouraging slave-morality. The sentimental liberties taken in literature and art and poetry that have grown up around the teachings of Christ are merely an example of complete misunderstanding of what this tremendous and ruthless teaching meant."

THE WORK

There is a common element in most religious teachings, ancient ones as well as New Age metaphysical ideologies and many popular belief or developmental systems, that is absolutely wrong. This is another way that the Work is very different from other paths. Almost all popular developmental systems teach that spiritual growth results in material world gains. This applies especially to wealth and health. The ideology is that higher consciousness or psychological/spiritual growth heals the physical body and provides wealth in the physical world. This is not correct. The material world cannot determine development in the metaphysical world. Anything can happen to your body and eventually everyone's body suffers and everyone's body dies. You need not allow your psychological state to depend upon your material world circumstances. You can develop Consciousness and Being regardless of your physical condition. This is a spiritual Truth and it is easily verifiable. General Observation of those who claim to have such development also easily shows that most are not rich in the world.

These ideas are misinterpreted even within legitimate systems. They are a lower level of understanding expressing a spiritual truth. And deliberately or not, they sell well. Tell people that all of their problems will be favorably resolved if they .... "whatever", and a lot of those people will try almost anything to gain the perfect health and perfect life they desire.

This is mixing different levels of Understanding. It is attributing to spiritual growth a corresponding material growth. It is saying that your worldly life will become perfect if your spiritual life becomes perfect. This is wishful thinking at best. Witness the lives of the saints. Anything can happen to anyone in life, including poverty and illness. But nothing can happen in life to anyone that can inhibit the development of Consciousness. Being, which is the expression of Consciousness, can accept life as it is, and continue to express and create and live in Goodness.

It is a serious mistake to believe that any particular path will result in perfect life in the physical world. The spiritual actualization of a person can happen regardless of life's circumstances, and this is the important point; if physical world gain is part or all of your motivation for being on a spiritual path you will develop nothing. The angle of approach is wrong and not accessible to the level of spirit. It makes your efforts conditional -- self-interested.

So this great lie, (and/or selling tactic), that followers of any particular teaching will have earthly superiority and powers, including health and wealth, seduces people away from the possibility of real spiritual transformation since real spiritual transformation means moving from egocentric psychology to self-transcendent psychology -- evolution.

If you reach the self-transcendent stage then you will see the partial truth which creates these misformulations. You will understand that a higher level of Consciousness and spiritual growth are the same thing. And that from a higher level of consciousness, spiritual understanding, the concerns of life change and your detachment with the circumstances of your life leave you content with what is. You are not as interested in what you can get or be, as in what you can give.

Real developed Being has patience and peace. It is content to wait or to act without requirements because living in Being is rich with meaning. Whether external life is difficult or easy remains irrelevant because your heart and mind are walking in the right path. That gives meaning to every day and the opportunity in every moment to be in the path, in this case to be in the Work.

This brings up another practice that is constantly misused and especially in Fourth Way schools. It is the practice of bringing your awareness to the present moment. If this psychological exercise is used correctly, it is a tool. Practicing correctly means precisely "bring your awareness into the present moment". This exercise will remove you from the mechanical momentum of life and your Identification with it. Instead of being totally Asleep and caught up in mechanical responses, you raise your awareness from that hypnotic state into cognizance of the present moment you are living. First, by sensing your body in the here and now and then by expanding your awareness to include your body in its surroundings and from your immediate environment to a broader scale. You notice that you feel tense, that your brow is furrowed or you are tapping your foot or your stomach is clenched, and you intentionally release the energy and relax. You deny any thoughts or emotions access to your attention which is focused in the moment. You look, you register, you release tension and you are not part of the mechanical stream of life for a few moments. You may feel a stronger sense of Real I as a result.

This is a valuable exercise that can take you out of the momentum of Sleep, give you an experience of scale and some awareness of Self outside of that mechanical momentum. It also gives the practitioner an experience of relief from identification "in the moment". It is this last part that has been perverted in Fourth Way instruction.

If you observe carefully you will see that the expansion of consciousness is horizontal, on the level of life in the world. It starts with becoming aware of yourself physically and expands to being aware of yourself contextually, physically. While this can provide valuable knowledge, it is a tool not an end. It is not the road to Conscious Evolution. It is one of many tools used to create a certain kind of awareness and in that, it is helpful. It does not create Real I, it clears the way for sensing it.

The misuse of this practice in the Fourth Way happens when a student gets addicted to the feeling of relief from Identification or painful emotion, even for a few moments. Or when the student is taught to use this practice to become Non-Identified whenever the student experiences Negative Emotions. Used in this way, it becomes an escape mechanism and does not allow the student the chance to Observe and recognize and separate from the Wrong Work that keeps creating the Negative Emotions. The student stays trapped in a blind alley when the experience of Negative Emotions is treated with this exercise. i.e. Negative Emotions = bring awareness to the physical world = temporary emotional relief = no clear Observation of what the Negative Emotion is and what it is connected to in the psychology = no means to deal with it or understand it or work against it to create transformation. So the student practicing wrongly cannot build a structure of Understanding that would eventually raise the student to a permanent place of Non-Identification. They can only try to jump up and touch that state over and over again. Touching that state is possible. Living in it requires building it. Building it requires attention and effort.

The Work gives us many tools and ideas with which to create transformation. The primary most essential exercise given is Self-Observation. It is through Self-Observation that you learn to see your own psychology functioning. You learn to "Know Thyself" through Self-Observation. It is the fundamental practice from which all development grows. In comparison, the exercise of being present provides little or no knowledge with which to Work.

In addition, the distortion of this practice is a devolution of an authentic exercise with sound intent. The right understanding of this psychological idea, which has gone so far down now that it is best expressed as "be here now", means something more like bringing your Real I into presence in the moment. It is a sacred practice and has nothing to do with the assertion of "I AM". The student who cannot manifest Real I, their own, is hardly in the position to utter the sacred " I AM" of the Creator and assign selfhood to it.

So this corrupted practice stops the developmental process and prevents the student from gaining the understanding received through Self-Observation. It also keeps the student enslaved to the "school", dependent upon it to provide the circumstances and Third Force to create an experience that mimics a higher conscious state and gives them great relief.

This relates to another distortion which is sold in Fourth Way schools and it appeals to the emotional suffering each person experiences. Sacrificing your suffering, learning how to become objective to it, detached from it, is not anything like emotional disassociation which is the result of wrong practicing. Emotional disassociation is the wrong work of the Emotional Center and severely limits your ability to receive the Work. Through the active process of the Work you will learn what Unnecessary Suffering is and become free of it. But the idea is sold that higher consciousness is free of suffering. This is not true. In some ways it suffers less, in some ways it suffers more. The idea of Non-Identification is clarity in the Emotional Center, not detachment from it.

This brings us to another serious distortion in most successful Fourth Way schools. The idea is that of "payment" and the distortion is again assigning literal meaning to a psychological truth. The "schools" teach that you have to pay for what you receive, specifically in money or services, to the "school". The principal is that if you pay money for it, you will value it more.

The idea that you have to pay for what you receive is accurate when understood psychologically. The Truth of this spiritual truth is that in order to gain in Consciousness or Being, i.e. evolve, you must sacrifice something, give something away. The principle behind it is that you must give up something internally in order to make room for the developing Consciousness. If you cling to the conditions that keep consciousness asleep and you give up nothing, then change is impossible. Without sacrifice there is no space internally for growth and change.

Consequently, there is Objective Truth in the idea that each person must make a "payment" in order to receive from the Teaching. The psychological Truth in the Work is that your "payment" is the effort you make, each effort you make, to Awaken. When, for instance, you have sacrificed your need to be right, what you receive is the freedom from the psychological tyranny of always having to be right. This is the correct Work understanding of payment and receipt.

This brings up a critical idea in the Work which must be understood correctly or no development is possible. Sacrifice. In almost every teaching, this idea is used to squeeze volunteerism and cash out of the student. You must sacrifice your time and energy to contribute to the community through manual labor or services and of course you must contribute money, and a particular amount at that, whether or not you can afford it.

Without saying that these kinds of sacrifices have no potential value, it is critical to understand that what the Work asks you to sacrifice is your suffering; that is, your Unnecessary Suffering. This is not a process that includes emotional disassociation (i.e., do not feel your emotions). Self- Observation will illuminate for you everything that you have to sacrifice, and the difference between Unnecessary Suffering and Necessary Suffering -- Self-Observation with Work knowledge and nothing else.

The whole idea of sacrifice has been so polluted with perversions that it is a vital concern that you understand that in the Work you make sacrifices by making the effort to apply the ideas to yourself. That effort may include gaining knowledge, opening your mind, directed thinking, intentional use of your attention and energy, actually practicing the psychological exercises, sincerity, dedication, Self-Observation, Inner Separation, Non-identification, External Considering, and much more. The ideas of Self-Observation, Inner Separation, Non-Identification, and External Considering are so dense that it is only through the experiential Verification of these practices that you can understand what they mean. Then, you will begin to understand what you need to sacrifice and how you can sacrifice. The first thing that you will understand is that this sacrificing is a psychological/spiritual exercise, not a physical world directive.

If you take this idea of sacrifice externally, that is exoterically, it is simple math to see that "the bigger the sacrifice, the bigger the gain", becomes the axiom. This level of understanding renders every perversion from poor people sending their life savings to televangelists, to intentionally creating suffering in order to make friction to generate a bigger sacrifice and even to literal human sacrifice of human life, and any other sick way individuals can create to avoid having to do the kind of real sacrificing necessary in the Work. The sacrifice of almost every external thing is always easier (the path of least resistance) than the sacrifice of ego, Acquired Personality, of Pictures you have of yourself, of Inner Considering, of Identification with Acquired Personality. It is easier and it is dangerous. Beware of religions, schools, developmental paths or systems that ask you to sacrifice your money and your time in service to them. They have either misunderstood something fundamental about real Conscious development or they are knowingly misusing this idea for their own gain. If you Work right and sacrifice right and have actual psychological transformation, then you will want to give back to what has given this miracle to you. At this point inspiration will let you know how to give back and it will be different for everyone, and money need not necessarily be part of that inspiration.

ON AIM

This next is an important point I want to emphasize. The Work is universally applicable because of the nature of Objective Truth. And, while I will continue to speak in Work terminology, do not forget that this System is called Esoteric Christianity -- by Gurdjieff, by Ouspensky, by Nicoll. That means that it is about the inner teaching of Christian transformation. Part of the brilliance of the Work is that it can be used and applied with the same results with or without any particular religious affiliation. However, these ideas taken out of the context of their Aim, that is to produce conscious evolution of Being (i.e. Goodness), can produce all varieties of distortions and perversions. Many of you have verified this for yourselves. In context, the dark places in the Work are not so frightening when you understand that the Aim is illumination; the confusing areas aren't as unstable when you know that Mercy accompanies you.

The possibility of every student's psychological evolution depends entirely upon the efforts they make. If you persevere in the Work sincerely, your aims will change, your motives will change and you will find that the result of doing the Work is Humility. Higher Consciousness is accessible through Humility.
Be sure that this is your Aim. That your motive for being in the Work is to achieve self-transcendent Being, which is Goodness. Otherwise your time and efforts will be wasted. If you believe that you already possess Consciousness and Humility, then you will not even want to do the Work or believe you need to. If you seek personal power in the world through the Work, you will find that it will not function in that way.

But if you seek to become the highest possibility of yourself, the best person you can be, authentic and good in your life, then -- that is here and now -- you are given the means. By some rare circumstances you have each been given the miraculous opportunity to come into contact with the Work. What you do with this unique gift is given to each of you to decide.

THE PATH TO EVOLUTION

Observe that the energy of life driving everything is Negativity, the "law of accident," mechanics producing predictable responses, everyone's total identification with every event, and therefore complete lack of relativity equals (Sleep). Injustice exists because of sleep.
There is another level of being that includes an increased perspective and understanding born of effort and experience in the Work. It includes relativity, compassion, and acceptance. Its nature is not that of self-interest and consequently it is liberated and can be objective, clear, and unidentified. Such observation is not emotionally dead or repressed, but serene and wise.
This is what is created through doing this inner Work. The psychological practices and ideas gradually clear away all the

wrong work of mechanical psychology (the lies and dirt of negativity in all its forms, self-interest, vanity, inner considering, pictures of oneself, lying, pride and everything else the Work tells us to observe). This process strips the personality (ego)and leaves you feeling vulnerable and rather without a "real personality" to replace the dying False Personality. You do not become withdrawn.

This is a critical stage in the Work. What this emptiness should create in you is humility. Not self-condemnation, but self-transcendence and real Self-Remembering. Humility expands understanding which imparts meaning.

A new Self is born with observing "I". It is the Real Self and will grow stronger and become more present with the continued practice of Self-Observation. With practical work and verifying experience, your awareness expands. Continuing sincere efforts can expand one's consciousness permanently, but what you sacrifice to reach this point is all that you believe yourself to be and all interest in seeking personal gratification. Not everyone is willing to pay such a high price.
Those who are courageous enough to continue will find valuation of the Work to be the only third force needed. Therefore, the new faculty in one's psychology (that of developing consciousness) is fed by the power of right valuation.

The path of evolution is upward toward illumination, through the sight of understanding, toward finer and finer energies that cannot support the weight of violence. This path leads away from the automatic animal level of being toward enlightened intentionality.

EVOLUTION

The idea of the possible evolution of a person by way of the Work means a development of consciousness which is implicitly accompanied by a corresponding development of Being. It is a psychological system and it is your psychology that changes. The results of this change eventually become spiritual development.

The Work psychological practices and ideas purify your psychology of self-interested motivations and requirements and negative emotions. These negative emotions make your inner life toxic and so full of noise that you are unable to hear or receive from anything higher than the mechanical level of Being. So you will be stuck in sleep until the obstruction of Negative Emotions has been removed.

In the case of the Work, the process involves transcendence, not repression of Negative Emotions. Self-transcendence is above the level of Negative Emotions and requires intentional effort until it becomes a permanent state. In Observing you will begin by noticing how often you feel Negative Emotions and have negative thoughts. You will see that your day begins with complaining or anxiety or worry or negative imagination, impatience, rushing, irritation, frustration. You will observe that you always do the same things and say the same things and respond in the same way to particular circumstances -- traffic, waiting in line, feeling offended, dissatisfaction, etc. You will clearly see insincerity in yourself. You will observe yourself, that is your Acquired Personality, lying frequently to others and to yourself by omission and by manipulating the facts, by misrepresenting something to save face, to be polite out of fear or insecurity for personal gain or by pretending anything. You will observe how Vanity and the imaginary Pictures you have of yourself, which are made of Vanity, are false and empty and they govern everything you do because you must maintain your particular idea of who you are. This is called Identification with yourself. You will see the falseness and feel the strength of Identification without being able to change it until you have Worked with it for a long time.

When you first begin to observe your Multiplicity, you will be confused about what is real and what is unreal among the Many I's. This is psychologically disorienting at first. It can be frightening but does not need to be. If you understand that you are given the opportunity to change certain aspects of yourself by way of being able to see them, then recognizing Multiplicity is a gift not a threat. If you can manage to practice Self-Observation uncritically at this time and let Conscience inform you about the I's you observe then the false, inauthentic harmful ones can be eliminated. It requires diligent practice and great courage and integrity within yourself to do the hard labor of purifying your Emotional Center.

The Work is ongoing and when you have conquered one aspect of Wrong work, you will find that there is another that needs Work effort. The Work will go deeper and your motives will become purer.

ON THE PROCESS

In the beginning a person has all of their attention directed outward mechanically. They are not aware of this because they are completely identified with themselves and with outer life.

Now when such a person first hears the ideas of the Work, let's suppose they feel a resonance inside with something like Conscience, Objective Truth, Recognition, Understanding. Even still, it is hard to credit that you are asleep, mechanical, an automatic stimulus-response organism and so is the entire rest of humanity. But Magnetic Center, Intellect, a glimpse of Understanding or an experience of Higher Consciousness urges you to concede the possibility of something very valuable, if as yet unarticulated.

So you begin to study the ideas of the Fourth Way and at once you hear that your attention, which has been entirely engaged with the external world, can be divided so that you may also be observing your internal world. You recognize an entirely new possibility. If you credit this idea and attempt to divide your attention and observe yourself, you find that there is something in you that can SEE (Observe). With practice, Self-Observation creates the presence of Observing I. Observing I has a Work Memory that becomes filled with verifications of Work ideas, pictures you have of yourself, photographs of Imagination, False Personality and Wrong Work.

Observing I becomes the seat of "Steward" -- a permanent faculty that receives the impressions from life, internal and external, through a level of Understanding informed by the Work ideas. Observing I has also been informing Real I, which grows from this Understanding and gains strength through practice and definition in contrast to Imaginary I. This Real I forms at the expense of or through the elimination of acquired Personality (False Personality), that is, your ego.

Real I seeks to exert control over Personality in order to be authentic, in order to replace Wrong Work with Right Work. As False Personality is observed and studied and worked against, it loses power, refuses to function, and eventually dissolves, vanishes to be replaced by your True Self, awakened, intentional, internally free, authentic, unique, purified of the labyrinth of Wrong Work, self-interest, and the Negative Emotions connected to them. Real I can "Know" because it is connected to Higher Consciousness, Objective Conscience. It has perfect integrity and contains the meaning and fulfillment of your existence.

PROGRESSION IN THE WORK

-- Divided Attention
-- Self-Observation
-- Recognizing mechanics and Sleep
-- Inner Separation
-- Non-Identification
-- The elimination of Inner Considering
-- The end of the wrong work of Emotional Center
-- Self-Remembering
-- The emergence of Real I
-- The formation of a permanent faculty that sees the world

through Work ideas verified and understood
-- Ongoing Self-Observation moving deeper
-- The change of perspective from Higher Consciousness
-- Forgiveness "happens" through Understanding
-- External Considering manifests
-- Developed Conscience directs actions
-- The freedom from False Personality
-- The authority and Will of True Personality
-- Increased valuation of the Work
-- With the purification of the Emotional Center comes
the receptivity, openness, flexibility, honest goodness and
the ability to "know" and "see" and "do" what is good and right
from the point of view of Higher Consciousness and Objective
Truth
-- The fulfillment of Meaning in your life

PART II

TEACHINGS

1

SELF-OBSERVATION

Self-observation is the foundational effort in this process, its value cannot be overestimated. All development proceeds from that point. You must intentionally turn a portion of your attention inward in order to observe yourself. It is essential not to judge or criticize what you observe in yourself. These emotions will distort what you observe and inhibit your progress.

***

Try to detach from your justifying and observe the feeling objectively. Keep tracking back, in your psychology not your history, to find the source of this unpleasant experience.

Continued self-observation will give you knowledge, understanding, and the possibility of detachment and liberation from this recurring state in you.

All wrong work loses force when it is seen through self-observation. Use the recognition of this unpleasant experience as your "reminding factor" and third force to not identify. You are then using the problem to solve the problem.

***

Before pursuing self-remembering, you must develop the skill of self-observation. There is a vast difference between self-observation and self-remembering. The latter is a higher state of Consciousness not an activity and it cannot be forced into existence. The basis of the Work is self- observation, not self-remembering. This is the only way to make
progress in the Work, namely through this persistent effort of seeing what you are and why you function the way you do.

***

Self-observation needs to be free-wheeling and spontaneous.
Your observations will lead to a catalog of insights
about yourself which will then give you a truer picture of what you have to work with. A journal might help keep track of these perceptions. But the heart of the effort is in the liberation from the prison of sleep.

Keep the Work efforts more internal.

***

Practice self-observation uncritically. Do not become identified with what you observe. Try to separate psychologically from all negative thoughts, states, and feelings. Release anxiety, let personality be passive, and observe, observe, observe.

***

It is true that we need to be "merciless" with ourselves in seeing things for what they are (namely, internal reactions, attitudes, states). But this mysterious practice of self-observation is about creating a new quality of awareness within yourself, and clearing the ground for a new sense of identity. Ultimately, it leads to a development of being that is characterized by great compassion, even for the mechanical and chaotic aspects of yourself.

So this is imperative: do not judge what you see, just see it. The more you see it, the more you will want to change it and the more opportunities will arise to do so.

Remember that this is not the way of self-denial, but of understanding. As you know, understanding is defined in the Work as the result of knowledge and being. Self-observation gives you knowledge on how to create being.

***

Your repeated efforts at self-observation will build a Work memory that
will in turn remind you to do the Work.

***

Self-observation is the primary psycho-transformational exercise given to us in the Work. All progress in the Work depends on diligent, uncritical, long-term self-observation. It is only through the experiential practice of this idea that one can gain the knowledge and understanding necessary for growth and change.

It is possible through self-observation to eventually gain control over your mechanics, to be liberated from unnecessary suffering, to find authentic personality, to be able to be intentional in your actions and form a body of Work I's that have a permanent Work perspective in you.
This Work is about personal internal purification. All the transforming knowledge in the Teaching is aimed at this goal of purifying the emotional center. Self-observation is necessary to shine the light of consciousness into the dark unconscious of our own psychology.

***

Regarding your statement on "surrendering my will":
Practicing the exercise of self-observation is not the same as

surrendering your will. Self-observation is the only source of information that will inform you about what you need to surrender and what you need to keep. So leave the surrendering of your will out of self-observation. Simply observe yourself non-critically and especially observe negativity.

***

The aim here is to see the psychological origins and motivations for our actions in the world.

***

In doing the Work, beginning with self-observation, little by little we disempower those tyrannical I's. We create in ourselves a place of knowledge, perspective, and empowerment from which we can act intentionally. As self-centered I's lose power under the effect of the Work (through the force of self-observation) we cease to have so many requirements of the world. We become free of constantly needing what we don't have, or constantly being unhappy with what we do have.

We recognize that our attitudes and opinions are relative and our likes and dislikes are irrelevant to reality. So it is essential to see yourself objectively or you will not recognize what it is you must work on. Remember that this Work is psychological and internal, requiring real and continued effort.

***

The reason that self-observation needs to be spontaneous is because you can only do it when it occurs to you, whenever and whatever the circumstances. The observing I will give you better information if it is unencumbered by schedule or contrivance.

***

What you need to be observing is what state you are in -- Are you confused? Are you anxious? Are you in negative imagination? Are you inner considering? Are you being critical of what you observe?

Do you notice when you are insincere? Do you see yourself lying, pretending to know, care, understand, be sympathetic, etc.? Can you feel identification when you are in it? Do you see changing I's? Contradictions between I's? Buffers?

Do you see vanity? The need to be right? Insisting on having your own way? Being disappointed that you don't have what you want? Do you notice how much of your behavior is based on what you like or don't like?

The point of all this OBSERVATION is to build Real I which is not polluted by any of the wrong work mentioned above. It takes intentional efforts, real desire for change, willingness to see yourself honestly, and time. This Work is a process that begins with the first I of self-observation and can grow to the point where there is a permanent presence in your psychology, a source of understanding formed by Work, knowledge and experience.

You say you forget constantly and ask if it is just a matter of will. It is a matter of building will. If you have an aim to observe yourself, your aim has force -- use it. Fill your life and your schedule with reminding factors, for example: put your wristwatch on the opposite wrist to remind yourself to observe every time you look at the wrong wrist. Put notes on mirrors and refrigerators, change patterns of activities to knock you out of your habitual routines.

***

Purifying the emotional center, "cleansing the cup", is the purpose of the Work and its results. This is achieved by diligent, humble efforts to see and detach from what is false, negative, and selfish in ourselves. Negative and judgmental attitudes will distort the seeing and keep you from the objective reality available only in non-identification.

***

In practicing self-observation, self-loathing is difficult to avoid. Being a negative emotion, it is necessary to avoid this in order to grow in the Work properly. To observe uncritically is so important in this process because it is through detachment (non-identification) that we are liberated. It is a waste of energy and wrong work of the emotional center to loathe what is only the manifestations of acquired personality.

***

Everyone comes into the Work with their personality, in full force. It is the condition sleeping humanity lives in. The work of self-observation, which is foundational in the process, requires intentional effort. Included in this intentionality is the practice of being uncritical about what you observe. If your observing I responds with hating what it sees, then that is where you will be stuck, in a constant war between the observer and the observed.

The whole point of self-observation is to give an objective view of what you are really like. Without objectivity, you are not going to see anything. Keep Observing I passive. That effort is part of making the effort to observe.

***

A new Self is born with observing "I". It is the Real Self and will grow stronger and become more present with the continued practice of self-observation. With practical work and verifying experience, your awareness expands. Continuing sincere efforts can expand your consciousness permanently, but what you sacrifice to reach this point is all that you believe yourself to be and all interest in seeking personal gratification. Not everyone is willing to pay such a high price.

***

QUESTION:

I seem to experience self-remembering more than I do self-observation. There are very frequent moments when I am painfully aware of myself, but do not know what to make of any of it.

RESPONSE:

Being painfully aware of yourself is neither self-remembering nor self-observation. It is the natural condition of every human being's psychology. It is inner considering. It is due to the wrong work of the emotional center that is concerned with "appearances" and other people's feelings toward you.

You are at the point where you are AWARE of being "painfully aware". This is a step above merely BEING "painfully aware". The next step is to simply be aware.

Just being "aware" is the first crack in the false personality. The Work starts here. Self-observation comes first. It is an intentional effort. It is done uncritically. Eventually, Observing I gains enough power to direct behavior. But for a long time you cannot do anything but observe.

***

What can you observe objectively about being irritable? Is it an unpleasant feeling or do you picture yourself as a "lovable grouch"? (There is no such thing, by the way). Are there any I's that secretly enjoy the zing of negative energy? What I's are irritable? The ones that want something that they don't have, the ones that have to do something that they don't want to do, the ones that are feeling inadequate, unsatisfied, unsure? We could go on and on, but the point is that all of the above and more belong to inner considering, to acquired attitudes, likes and dislikes, etc. That is ALL that the Work tells us that we must separate from.

Knowing this can give you the force to become detached and in that state of non-identification see clearly what intentional right action is. Then you lose all motivations and justifications for being irritable.

So, how do you know if you are observing yourself through a filter of false personality? If Observing I is objective, non-identified, then false personality CANNOT be present. One must work at this also, making Observing I not react with identification. This is difficult work as well, but it leads to liberation, to that escape from the prison of sleep that we seek.

Ouspensky was right about needing help. We need the help of knowing a way out and the help of someone who knows also that "way" from experience and can assist you through the difficulties and help you avoid the traps. Someone who really knows the way can help you to verify for yourself the ideas of the Work and their transformative power.

To be absolutely sure that your work is progressing in the proper direction is easy. Follow goodness. Seek to act with unself-interested intentionality. Every normally formed human being has the innate knowledge (faculty of recognition) of what GOODNESS is. The Truth in it resounds in your soul with recognition.

***

The process of self-observation requires intentional, repeated efforts over a long period of time, and it is often genuinely painful work. We learn that we spend most of our time in some kind of negative state and from an objective point of view we see the unnecessary suffering of it, the wrong work of it, the interference of it and the loss of energy that it costs us. These ideas are strong motivations for change. We see our own automatic behavior which may shock and humiliate us and we are helpless to do anything about it at first. We recognize that every action is motivated by self-interest. We see in ourselves lying, justifying, manipulating, attention-seeking, competitiveness, vanity, the falsehood of pictures we have about ourselves, the multiplicity of acquired personality, even the corruption of merit seeking in our good works.

When the light of self-observation begins to reveal our inner states and psychological condition, the Observing I is still too weak to change anything it observes. However, repeated observations steal power from identifying with our mechanics, help us to separate from them and form a stronger Observing I which eventually does have the power to affect change.

This is a process of purification which removes the obstacles that cut us off from the state of self-remembering. The goal is the formation of a permanent Real I which is the manifestation of the state of self-remembering. Self-observation, founded on divided attention, creates the link between self-remembering and the development of Real I.

***

It is only natural in the developmental process of the Work that in the beginning the power of your personality is much stronger than your will or ability to remain conscious or internally aware. At first, when you try to practice self-observation, you can only get glimpses of the external reality and the internal reality at the same time. You may find it helpful to reflect upon any effort of self-observation after the fact, picturing it from an objective, external point of view where you can see the event, where you are cognizant of your own inner state and detached from both (or not identified with either). These glimpses and reflections form photographs for you. They give you information that you can verify through further observations. The attention that is directed toward your psychology becomes Observing I. Observing I grows with every photograph and every verification of Work knowledge. Eventually, Observing I has the Will to remain conscious.

***

The Work asks you to note your state. This indeed requires great effort. That's why it is called Work. But it is possible to do it (practice self-observation in this manner) and you don't have to take my word for it. You can verify it for yourself through your own experience. Of course, you have to make the effort of self-observation repeatedly in order to build something strong enough inside you to observe yourself as a regular activity. This will take much work and a long time. So evaluate your aim in undertaking the Work.

If you decide to do this Work, your efforts will create a response that enlightens you.

***

I must point out that Self-Observation is a specific psychological exercise that is unique to the Work. It is not practice of the present moment or paying attention to anything other than your own psychological processes and states.

What you are seeing when you experience yourself as "simply a bundle of tape recordings and reactions responding from these" is False Personality. It is relevant because it makes up your present reality. You do have a True Self which doing the Work will lead you to discover. The process of discovery begins with relentless practice of self-observation. It is imperative that one is uncritical of what is observed.

You are not only programs and mechanics. There is something in you that is authentic, unique behind all of these things. That Real I, True Self begins to gain strength or surface with the first observation of False Personality. Since you know already that there is something in you that isn't only mechanical, the I that knows this is the I of self-observation. That I is the beginning of who you are (Real I).

Once you have observed in yourself (verified) that Sleep and Mechanicalness and False Personality exist not only in you but also in everyone else, it becomes easier to forgive BECAUSE you understand the nature and the power of Sleep. This helps to reinforce Real I which will then give you more power to forgive and understand.

***

When you first begin to practice Self-Observation, you will probably begin with seeing yourself as if from a distance. In other words, you will see yourself constantly touching your hair or shoving your fists deep into your pockets, or flirting, or not looking someone in the eye, or posturing in any of the different ways we all do. Or you may first notice that a particular state is always created by the same and repeated circumstances; as soon as you get in the car you become tense, anticipating the drive ahead, or having a particular activity interrupted you notice that you always become irritated. Or receiving mail, e or otherwise, gives you a little thrill, a compliment makes you feel validated, happy. But all of this is only half the picture, the external half.

The other part of this practice is to begin to see your internal states and psychology as well, and in conjunction with your external observances. It may begin as only an awareness, for instance you "see" yourself acting very self-confidently while you are actually feeling insecure. Or you observe yourself in conversation nodding apparently in agreement or understanding, when you actually have no idea what the other person is talking about.

Self-Observation does take effort and it requires long-term, often repeated efforts. Sometimes you will see something very clearly, sometimes your efforts produce nothing or something vague, or only later will you become cognizant of what was observed earlier.

But when you begin to make sincere and repeated efforts to observe yourself, you will probably experience what your fellow student did. You will have a spontaneous experience of Self-Observation that will feel clearer to you because there is only seeing, without trying. This happens because what practices Self-Observation in you is Observing I and it is growing in presence with every experience of Self-Observation.
Eventually, after long-term authentic Work, Self-Observation becomes a sort of faculty in your psychology that functions on its own. It creates Observing I which becomes Real I which has

access to Objective Consciousness.

What effort is too great to make for this?

***

When I speak of Self-Observation, I am not referring to Self-Remembering. These are two distinct and very different experiences and practices. Self-Observation is psychological exercise of seeing objectively both our inner state and our outer reality at the same time. It is an exercise that over a long period of time and a large accumulation of observations leads to a degree of self knowledge and objectivity (non-identification). Under these conditions, Self-Remembering can take place.

***

Knowledge in the Fourth Way means understanding the Work ideas. That requires "pondering" AND practical Work. Increase your efforts to gain all the intellectual information you want or need, and reflect upon it. Then begin the initial practices of Self-Observation and not expressing Negativity. That is the process for Awakening. And that's a long one. If you are just beginning in the Work, presume nothing. Verify everything. Read, read, read and practice Self-Observation, and we will help you with any questions or difficulties you have along the way.

***

When you are practicing Self-Observation and that which you are trying to observe disappears, there are a couple of possible explanations. In the beginning, although it may seem hard to grasp, the ego will oppose Work efforts. It does not want to change and it certainly doesn't want to be seen. So perhaps some particular I's are hiding from observation. Sometimes when you practice Self-Observation that which is observed simply ceases to exist under the light of observation. For instance, if you are angry and you observe your anger in the context of Work knowledge and you see the self-interest, the lie, the machinations, the childishness in the anger, it can die on the spot. It isn't a should or shouldn't situation. This is just one of the things that occurs during Self-Observation.

You have a very important opportunity in what you have been experiencing. You say "the emotional feeling is separated from the thoughts that have aroused these feelings". The thoughts are only I's and separating them from the emotional feeling that they evoke is what we work very hard to be able to do. To have experienced this spontaneously is an insight and maybe an organic understanding of that condition of inner separation that can help to know what you are aiming at. It is freedom from Identification.

To remain objective during Observation takes practice. It may help you to separate the Observing I from your personality's manifestations by referring to them in your observations as "it" rather than taking them as yourself. For instance, "it" (meaning the mechanical, automatic personality that you call "self") is irritable. It feels successful. It is tired. It doesn't like...It thinks that people should...Some people find this exercise helpful.

You could try, while being externally aware, to have Observing I passively registering what it sees, maybe only subconsciously sensing the inner state. In other words, you see yourself talking to someone and your Observing I just notes that you are uncomfortable. Let it go. Reflect on it later. Remember that what you are observing, the manifestations of your False Personality, is not you. It is the acquired attitudes, opinions, likes, dislikes, pictures and imaginations, habitual behaviors, habitual thought processes that were laid down in you without your conscious participation. All of these things are not what is real in you. When you know this, it becomes easy for Observing I to be objective. It is not the real you that is being observed. What is behind the Observer is the Real you. It is through Self-Observation that Real I comes into existence and gains Consciousness and Will.

***

So you begin by observing passively, externally and internally, and you begin to see the contradictions between external behavior and internal states and notices that the internal state is always some variation of self-interest; the need to be noticed, appreciated, treated well, the desire to be understood, to possess abilities that others value, the need to be right, the feeling of embarrassment and insecurity when these needs and desires aren't met; the bragging and preening of Vanity; the insincere salaciousness of flirting; lying overtly and lying covertly by pretending to be interested, pretending to know when you don't, pretending to care when you don't, pretending to listen when in reality your mind is on something else entirely; manipulations and the inauthentic actions of all varieties. Inner Considering is always concerned with how it appears. This is only sometimes Vanity. External appearances, position, appropriate deference, merit, status, valuation are all core emotions in Inner Considering.

It is only by observing, verifying and working against Inner Considering that one can begin to get to the point where your every thought and action is not motivated by self-interest. This is where real External Considering can begin to happen. It doesn't happen by focusing exclusively on the thoughts

2
DIVIDED ATTENTION

QUESTION:

We have given ourselves a task where we sense our body (our right hand)while we listen or talk with another. Or even just while we do our job. We find we can have an overall "awakened" sense with this divided attention but, it quickly turns into a time when attention begins to switch back and forth between hand and subject. Are these mini identifications? Would this be time to stop the task and come back or try to work through it?

RESPONSE:

The purpose of these exercises in divided attention is to prove that divided attention exists. It is possible. It is actually a big accomplishment to verify divided attention, even if it happens only in small doses. And it will come in small doses for a very long time. The ability to divide your attention for longer periods of time comes with practice.

However, you have already proved that you CAN divide your attention. You no longer need to waste this effort on any pointless activity. Now you need to direct one part of your attention not toward your body or any other external thing, but inward toward observing your own psychology while the other part stays engaged in the world.

When you first direct your attention inward, try only to observe what is going on, to register negative states, incongruities, inner considering, vanity, inner talking, insincerity, etc. Try not to react, criticize or judge what you observe.

This is the beginning of psychological transformation, to see your own psychology in action, to "know thyself". Read and study what the Work teaches about sleep, multiplicity, mechanicalness and all else one must observe and verify internally. Each observation is a step in the growth of Real I, so don't waste the effort of dividing your attention on externals. Observe YOURSELF with your divided attention.

* * *

Before a person learns that there is a practice called Divided Attention, and before they can Understand how to use this practice to see within themselves Objectively, no such idea exists in them that there is something other than what they call "I". When I teach someone to separate their thought processes into two different streams of direction, if I do not keep them on the right path in the right direction, this dichotomy in their mind can seem just like a schizophrenic state, that is, they lose their sense of themselves. Those here can attest to the difficulty of this stage. That makes me responsible for seeing to it that each student passes through this stage undamaged and can progress to fulfillment in the Work.

***

Working with Divided Attention not specifically related to Self-Observation is a waste of time. It can be a subject of fascination for the psychology and many people will prefer to remain at this kindergarten stage of practice rather than apply what has been learned to themselves.

***

Continuing to practice exercises of divided attention without using that divided attention to observe yourself is a wasted effort. Once you can divide your attention, then turn that part of it to psychological Work practices that can get you somewhere beyond dividing your attention. No matter what other Work efforts you make, if you are not practicing the psychological exercises regularly of true Self-Observation, Inner Separation, Non-Identification, the Stop exercise, External Considering, then no growth can happen.

Divided Attention precedes and is necessary for Self-Observation, but it is not Self-Observation. You cannot observe yourself without dividing your attention but Self-Observation is a specific practice in and of itself.

The beginning of divided attention is realizing that your attention goes in one direction only -- outward -- and that you live only in response to external stimuli. The "I" that can recognize this is the first "I" of divided attention. The point of the effort is that through realization and practice you can now have more than one perspective.

For instance, the practice of seeing a tree and seeing yourself seeing a tree is useful only in so far as it confirms that one CAN have divided attention. The aim is to take part of the attention that is normally directed outward, engaging in life, and turn that attention inward to see your behavior and the psychology that generates it from an objective perspective.

If you can do this, then you are using divided attention in order to practice self-observation. The aim of self-observation is to uncritically observe your psychology and your behavior in relation to Work knowledge. The Work tells us our behavior is governed by mechanics, that we are all asleep and furthermore that we do not know that we are asleep. The overall purpose of self-observation is awakening. In awakening we see what motivates our behavior, we learn how to become intentional, self-transcendent, and authentic.

The Work begins with dividing one's attention. If you have had no experience in this practice, try the following:
While being aware of your external experience become concurrently aware of your inner state. This internal awareness is the beginning of self-observation.

* * *

QUESTION:

I recall Ouspensky saying that in the practice of Divided Attention, the attention is shared between the 'observer and the observed'...

RESPONSE:

Divided Attention keeps us aware of our external circumstances while noticing our internal states. The central issue is seeing what is going on within you so that --

a) you are not completely controlled by it
b) you begin to understand why you function the way you do
c) you begin the process of changing your ways of being and reacting.

***

QUESTION:

How is Divided Attention different from remembering oneself while looking at an external object, where two lines are created, one towards the object and one towards the viewer?

RESPONSE:

Part of your attention is not caught up in the external flow of events. It sees your internal psychological condition.

The aim here is to see the psychological origins and motivations for your actions in the world . You have to start by seeing in yourselves what the Work tells you to observe.

You must make many observations over a long period of time before you can even begin to get a picture of what you have to work on. Remember that the aim of the Work is psycho-transformation.

Self-Remembering is not an exercise. It is a state. Sometimes you'll unexpectedly finds the state of Self-Remembering as a result of self-observation and inner separation. Sometimes this happens when you are observing yourself and you see that your outward manifestations are all driven by false personality and you have a moment of not knowing what you are besides that artificial personality. A sense of serenity and self undefined may be experienced in that moment. You may encounter something more authentic than what you are observing.

Real Divided Attention requires intentional effort for the specific purpose of self-observation. Trying to practice self-remembering while looking at an external object is a meaningless mind game. In order to remember oneself, it is first necessary to have observed oneself and created enough real Self to know what to remember. Therefore, in order to self-remember, you must first observe.

***

The beginning of Divided Attention is realizing that your attention goes in one direction only -- outward -- and that you live only in response to external stimuli. The "I" that can recognize this is the first "I" of Divided Attention. The point of the effort is that through realization and practice you can now have more than one perspective.

For instance, the practice of seeing a tree and seeing yourself seeing a tree is useful only in so far as it confirms that one CAN have Divided Attention. The aim is to take part of the attention that is normally directed outward, engaging in life, and turn that attention inward to see your behavior and the psychology that generates it from an objective perspective.

If you can do this, then you are using Divided Attention in order to practice self-observation. The aim of self-observation is to uncritically observe your psychology and your behavior in relation to Work knowledge.

***

The goal is the formation of a permanent Real I which is the manifestation of the state of self-remembering. Self-observation, founded on Divided Attention, creates the link between self-remembering and the development of Real I.

***

The purpose of these exercises in Divided Attention is to prove that Divided Attention exists. It is possible. It is actually a big accomplishment to verify Divided Attention, even if it happens only in small doses. And it will come in small doses for a very long time. The ability to divide your attention for longer periods of time comes with practice.

However, you have already proved that you CAN divide your attention. You no longer need to waste this effort on any pointless activity. Now you need to direct one part of your attention not toward your body or any other external thing, but inward toward observing your own psychology while the other part stays engaged in the world.

When you first direct your attention inward, try only to observe what is going on, to register negative states, incongruities, inner considering, vanity, inner talking, insincerity, etc. Try not to react, criticize or judge what you observe.

This is the beginning of psychological transformation, to see your own psychology in action, to "know thyself". Read and study what the Work teaches about sleep, multiplicity, mechanicalness and all else one must observe and verify internally. Each observation is a step in the growth of Real I, so don't waste the effort of dividing your attention on externals. Observe YOURSELF with your Divided Attention.

***

QUESTION:

Why should one begin with practicing Divided Attention? It has been my experience that one must first be able to direct their attention rather than having it taken away from them (day dreaming, identification, etc.). So, how can you practice Divided Attention if you don't have real attention?

RESPONSE:

Of course everyone has some degree of attention. It's just that it's scattered and constantly changing directions. But people do focus on work, on reading, entertainment, hobbies, etc. all the time. It may not be intentional, but it is directed. What the Work asks you to do is to focus part of it on one single thing: your inner reality. If you want to do pale exercises like seeing how long you can focus your attention on the second hand of your watch, you will indeed verify that it is nearly impossible to keep your thoughts from wandering for even a minute or two. It shouldn't take more than once or twice to learn that lesson.

But what if, for the sake of experimentation, you intentionally and repeatedly turn some bit of your attention that you can control toward the same thing, starting as an awareness of your inner state in the context of your outer circumstances at the moment. Maybe you're meeting someone new when you remember to observe your inner state; for a moment or two, you see yourself smiling, shaking hands, talking, etc. AND at the same time you are aware that inside you are feeling nervous or insecure, superior, inconvenienced, delighted, interested, afraid, sexually attracted, totally bored, or any other possibility.

The Work asks you to note your state. This indeed requires great effort. That's why it is called Work. But it is possible to do it (practice self-observation in this manner) and you don't have to take my word for it. You can verify it for yourself through your own experience. Of course, you have to make the effort of self-observation repeatedly in order to build something strong enough inside you to observe yourself as a regular activity. This will take much work and a long time. So evaluate your aim in undertaking the Work.

If you decide to do this Work, your efforts will create a response that enlightens you.

***

QUESTION:

I think the idea is that, as I pay attention to my surroundings, I am less absorbed in my internal mental world. Not wasting energy in imagination. Because it's hard to do both at once.

RESPONSE:

You seem to be stuck in the first movement of Self-Observation which is Divided Attention. This has no value except in application to the observation of your internal state. This Work is about your internal mental world. It requires that you place your attention there. In doing this, you are not in imagination, you are just beginning to observe (which is not absorption).

***

In the beginning of the Work there is a dangerous stage, when you instruct a person on how to practice Divided Attention and Self-Observation. This condition of Divided Attention and Self-Observation, if not done with very exacting parameters, can be schizophrenic inducing. So I would ask you please to take a very long time in practicing and understanding the Work before deciding what to share and how to share it with others.

***

Before a person learns that there is a practice called Divided Attention, and before they can Understand how to use this practice to see within themselves Objectively, no such idea exists in them that there is something other than what they call "I". When I teach someone to separate their thought processes into two different streams of direction, if they do not stay on the right path, aimed in the right direction, this dichotomy in their mind can seem just like a schizophrenic state, that is, they lose their sense of themselves. Those here can attest to the difficulty of this stage. That makes me responsible for seeing to it that each student passes through this stage undamaged and can progress to fulfillment in the Work.

3
IDENTIFICATION

Being able to see it- Identification is one of the most difficult
psychological aspects to Observe. When you are Identified,
Observing I isn't present. It takes more effort to Observe
Identification than to Observe the results of Identification...
Negative I's, complaints, Inner Considering, etc.

* * *

Identification is not an attention issue. It is the wrong work of the
emotional center.

***

A person attempting to awaken by way of the Work will be able to
have some small part of their mind SEE identification happening in
themselves. These I's that can see identification are not themselves
identified. Consequently, the force of identification is lessened by
the I's that can see it and refuse to give their energy to it. This is
a powerful incentive to practice self-observation and inner
separation.

The accumulated I's of observation and verification and
understanding eventually have enough force to stop automatic
emotions and reactions. The aim here being to consciously chose
right action.

Identification is especially hard to work on because we get our
sense of who we are by way of identifying, i.e. what you care
about, what you love, hate, need, want, etc. It fills you with energy
and a sense of meaning when it is really only stealing your life and

your force. Since we "feel" like we are defined by what moves us the most ("I'm a Republican, a victim, a freedom fighter, a feminist, a devout person), it is very difficult to see a level of relativity that denies one's sense of self and purpose. This is the stripping of the ego. It is painful and hard to let go of long-held convictions (identifications), to see with relativity that your attitudes, opinions, presumptions, and passions all have been acquired throughout your life. Therefore, they are subjective. They are changeable. They contain not the whole truth of a thing, only that which satisfies the false personality. They are not you.

Only inner separation, another difficult practice, can work at first against identification. Eventually, when the emotional center has been cleansed of the self-interest that builds identifications, action from a higher, more objective level is possible. You will be able to choose consciously what to give your energy to and how. But this is very far down the road. Be patient while Working. Results are usually a long time in coming, but growth is every step of the way.

Observe identification. See the strength of the grip that it has on you. See the same grip it has on others. See how it fills you with energy, how you get a little thrill from the jolt of it. See how it is full of justification. See that the agenda that fires your identification is self-serving and so is the next person's, and the next.

This is where to make personality passive. The "why" is so that you can see through the false personality and all its obstructions to a higher level of scale and relativity which can free you from identification.

Exercises to work on identification:

--self-observation
--register identification
--try to observe where it originates in you
--try to see its motivation
--practice inner separation
--practice the stop exercise

--make personality passive
--give no attention to justifying I's
--remember scale and relativity
--remember objective truth
--remember yourself

***

The burst of energy that you experienced ought to be a positive experience, sometimes accompanied by a flash of higher consciousness. This energy is liberated from the identification that would have consumed it. If there is not identification, that energy is available for something else.

***

The idea of "doing exercises to help build an observer and like what it didn't like" is only half right. One builds an observer through self-observation. Trying to like what it doesn't like is wrong work of the emotional center. The idea of trying to like what the machine doesn't like is more about separation and non-identification than it is about forcing yourself to endure something that is distasteful. It is also unnecessary and will inhibit real self-observation which must stay objective in order to work properly.

***

Wrong work of the emotional center results in wasted energy (can you afford it?) and is an obstruction to Higher Emotion and will foul up the workings of the other centers with hurry and identification, etc.

***

QUESTION:

Is identification the result of the dominant function of the emotional parts of the centers, particularly the emotional and intellectual centers? Is this why we are to make personality passive? Does it all boil down to fact that we have utterly no control over emotions? Are there exercises for bringing emotions under control?

RESPONSE:

Identification is the WRONG WORK of the emotional center. It can be active in any center. For example, the instinctive center is identified when it is denied the satisfaction it constantly seeks, i.e. meals on time, ample sleep, familiar surroundings, feeling safe...

The moving center gets identified with having to hold still, not having its hands busy, slow people, traffic.

The emotional center gets identified with everything because it responds to every event in life from the emotions. It empathizes without discretion, it loves or hates according to the dictates of false personality.

The intellectual center is identified when its ideas, understanding or presumptions are discredited or when it is challenged with problem-solving, when it seeks knowledge for power, or when it gets excited about learning something new.

The emotional center's real dominant function is emotional cognition. Your emotional center will tell you more about the nature of reality in any circumstance than any other center. The speed with which it works makes Working with the emotional center very difficult. But NOT impossible.

In a person asleep, the emotional center's wrong work is constantly moving from identification to inner considering and back (a person who is inner considering is identified with himself).

A person attempting to awaken by way of the Work will be able to have some small part of their mind SEE identification happening in themselves. These I's that can see identification are not themselves identified. Consequently, the force of identification is lessened by the I's that can see it and refuse to give their energy to it. This is a powerful incentive to practice self-observation and inner separation.

The accumulated I's of observation and verification and understanding eventually have enough force to stop automatic emotions and reactions. The aim here being to consciously chose right action.

Identification is especially hard to work on because we get our sense of who we are by way of identifying, i.e. what you care about, what you love, hate, need, want, etc. It fills you with energy and a sense of meaning when it is really only stealing your life and your force. Since we "feel" like we are defined by what moves us the most ("I'm a Republican, a victim, a freedom fighter, a feminist, a devout person), it is very difficult to see a level of relativity that denies one's sense of self and purpose. This is the stripping of the ego. It is painful and hard to let go of long-held convictions (identifications), to see with relativity that your attitudes, opinions, presumptions, and passions all have been acquired throughout your life. Therefore, they are subjective. They are changeable. They contain not the whole truth of a thing, only that which satisfies the false personality. They are not you.

Only inner separation, another difficult practice, can work at first against identification. Eventually, when the emotional center has been cleansed of the self-interest that builds identifications, action from a higher, more objective level is possible. You will be able to choose consciously what to give your energy to and how. But this is very far down the road. Be patient while Working. Results are usually a long time in coming, but growth is every step of the way.

Observe identification. See the strength of the grip that it has on you. See the same grip it has on others. See how it fills you with energy, how you get a little thrill from the jolt of it. See how it is full of justification. See that the agenda that fires your identification is self-serving and so is the next person's, and the next, though the identifications may oppose one another.

This is where to make personality passive. The "why" is so that you can see through the false personality and all its obstructions to a higher level of scale and relativity which can free you from identification.

***

You say "the emotional feeling is separated from the thoughts that have aroused these feelings". The thoughts are only I's, and separating them from the emotional feeling that they evoke is what we work very hard to be able to do. To have experienced this spontaneously is an insight and maybe an organic understanding of that condition of inner separation that can help to know what you are aiming at. It is freedom from Identification.

***

Identification is always the wrong work of the Emotional Center. It feels real because it is. You have given it reality by consenting to it. It also has a more intense energy than Non-Identification, which helps to make it feel more real. Identification helps create opinions, attitudes and convictions, likes and dislikes, which consequently make you think that it IS who you are. It is NOT. These attributes are acquired. They belong to False Personality. You are the Real I of your Higher Conscious Self; the authentic Self you are seeking to manifest.

***

Sometimes just seeing repeatedly the same manifestations of the wrong work of False Personality diminishes their strength. After all, the I's of Self-Observation are not identified with what is observed. As they accumulate, they draw force from Identification, weakening its hold on you, eventually giving you enough Will to disengage from wrong work.

***

I cannot think of any wrong work from the other centers, Intellectual, Moving, Instinctive, that isn't the product of the

Emotional Center's wrong work acting through the other centers. For instance, an avid reader who lives her life with her face in a book is definitely misusing the Intellectual Center. The Emotional Center is investing the Intellectual Center with energy that is out of place in that center. It creates fervor, it creates Identification, it creates an imbalance in the activity of the centers.

The wrong work of the Moving Center is almost always hurry - People who can't stop rushing and can't stop doing things, who can't sit still. This is caused by the Emotional Center acting inappropriately in the Moving Center, creating Identification and agitation.

Instinctive Center Wrong Work involves obsessive behavior of an instinctive nature, i.e. eating, sex, sleeping, etc.

***

Indeed Vanity can attach itself to anything, but the issue here has to do with the Work idea that thoughts come into you from all different sources -- some you can recognize, some you can't -- but any thought ("aren't I something!!") is just a passing I. You can credit it or not, you can identify with it or not, or you can ignore it. Ask yourself if this is a Real feeling that you have? Probably not, but if it is and you persevere in the Work, you'll lose that one fast.

***

Take the issues as they come up. When you notice that you are identifying again, STOP. If for instance you hate the drive to work, the traffic, waiting at lights, other drivers' behavior and negativity, the loss of productive time...you are driving (a moving centered activity) with your Emotional Center. Disengage your emotions from moving centered activity.

If you notice that what you are identifying with is a future event, then you are almost certainly in Imagination. Of course, directed, creative, intentional Imagination (how to work out a problem or create a particular outcome) is valuable, Intellectual Centered work. But you will probably find that your negative imagining is full of speculation and the negative discourse that accompanies it. This is Emotional Center's wrong work again, distorting the Intellectual Center's proper activity. If you have Work concerns, you can deal with them without identifying. Let your Emotional Center inform you, not steamroll you.

***

QUESTION:

I observed a moment that would usually lead to identification and imagination about the future. I noticed that a "want" internally arrived as a response to an internal 'emptiness'. This "want", should I have gone with it, would have fed me or filled me up in some way and conversely, should I be able to stay with the state of 'hunger' or 'emptiness' and not immediately react, I might avoid identification. Can you comment on this?

RESPONSE:

This experience of not going with an automatic I is crucial.. What it might have fed you would have been waste. If you can avoid identification, that would be the kind of emptiness that is serene and receptive. If the emptiness and hunger you experience are negative emotions, identify them as such and do not touch them psychologically.

***

QUESTION:

Ouspensky said that identification was the other side of the coin of self-remembering. Is this a useful characterization? Is identification wrong work of only the emotional center or all emotional parts?

RESPONSE:

Identification is the wrong work of the Emotional Center in any part.

Identification has more feeling in it than ordinary emotions.

People live by going from identification to identification. They define themselves by what they identify with.

Identification is emotional wrong work occurring in any center.

Being identified is automatic behavior. There is no consciousness in it. It is subjective and what is important to you at this time in your life can change in a New York minute.

Try to see Identification as an obstruction to clear observations.

***

Do you notice that what you identify with has strong emotions attached to the Identification? Question those emotions. What are they? What is their statement? Where do they come from? Name the source. Make them account for their identification. What do they say? Examine the Emotional Center for awareness that may be present and can inform you. Don't trust negative emotions.

***

If you write down over a period your I's that complain you will notice that you have the same complaint, let's say in regards to one person and you notice later that you have the same complaint about an entirely different person. This is an indication that the complaint is about something in you that you have not observed yet. You have only observed the result of it. It feels like you are in it because you are identified with it. This is what identification feels like.

***

QUESTION:

I often feel myself shifting out of Work I's and in to the other more common, automatic I's. I identify with them and feel that "this is me". This leads me to have an indifferent feeling toward the fewer work I's. I know that every moment, every reaction, every attitude, is an opportunity for self-observation. I feel that there are many opportunities to observe myself and that they are missed due to identification. I feel that if I "am" the I's then I cannot observe them.

RESPONSE:

This identification with yourself is false. What is habitual and mechanical feels natural. It is natural to the psychological functioning of man asleep. This man asleep is kept asleep through identifying with himself and therefore remains at a level that is actually sub-animal and unreachable by anything above it

***

The momentum of talking will reinforce Identifications. It will also keep you from accurate Self-Observation.

***

In the beginning Observing I identifies with everything. If you find it in identification with the Work, this is a good thing. It is when you begin to see and feel that you are not one I that you will discover that you can choose which I is real.

***

QUESTION:

Is not identification and imagination also wrong work of emotional center and would one student be more likely to fall into imagination rather than identification so in this way a student could be typed as to a chief fault?

RESPONSE:

Inner Considering is a form of Identification and Imagination always overlaps Identification. One student may be more vulnerable to one kind of wrong work over another, but the bottom line is that it is Wrong Work and must be eliminated.

***

Revenge is an extreme form of account making which belongs to Inner Considering which belongs to Identification. This long stream of wrong work that begins with Negativity created by Inner Considering can lead all the way to violence.

***

QUESTION:

Would it be right work of centers to proceed to "do what is necessary", in a practical sense, without investing the situation with emotion?

RESPONSE:

It would be the right work to do what is necessary without Identification. Identification is hyper-emotion.

***

Wrong Work atrophies under the influence of the light of Self-Observation and through the denial of Identification with it. Other elements come into play like thought selection and Inner Separation but a good deal of power exists in the light of Observing I.

***

QUESTION:

I think our experience in life comes from what we identify with.

RESPONSE:

It's more like what we identify with creates our experience of life.

That you are able to Observe and even prevent the expression of old Negative I's is an accomplishment even if you are inconsistent at it. But you have said it yourself: These very strong Identifications are convinced they are right and are firmly entrenched. That is the definition of Identification. It is consequently understandable that when you usurp an entrenched characteristic it leaves a vacuum and something that you felt very attached to disappears, leaving you with that feeling of no bearings. If you continue to practice as you have been, you will get to a point where you are so free from old Identifications and Pictures and Imagination about yourself that there will be no False Personality to quibble with. You can be and if you continue earnestly as you have been, you will be free of all of the Wrong Work that stands between where you are now and your full potential.

Your experience is random. It comes to you from outside of you and inside of you without purpose or direction. All kinds of experiences pass through your life. And one places the blame on external circumstances for these experiences? It is what you Identify with that creates what you feel is your experience. Your Identification with accidental associations is what attracts and holds your attention and makes you feel that your life is the result of Identification. When in fact it is what you Identify with among the many experiences that come to you which forms the content of your life.

***

Identification is not a barrier to Observing I.

***

QUESTION:

It is the same old reoccurrence going 'round and 'round and going nowhere.

RESPONSE:

All of these songs are Identification with yourself. And, as you know, Identification stops you dead in your tracks in the Work. They do go nowhere, but they use most of your energy getting there.

***

QUESTION:

What is it that does not Identify?

RESPONSE:

Real I. This is above the level of Identification.

***

Non-Identification should not hurt. Just the opposite. It should heal. When you can't Separate from an Negative Emotion, it needs further scrutiny. Try to discern what the I's of Identification are saying and determine whether they are true. If this escapes you at the time, practice Inner Silence in relation to your Identification. Do not listen to its I's. Do not speak to them. Do not acknowledge them. Reflection will inform you later about what the Identification was.

***

False Personality's strongest weapon is Identification. Fight it with detachment.

***

If you want to diffuse old accounts, begin with trying to see within yourself what Identifications initiated the account. In a general sense, the way to do this is to put yourself in the other person's place. See from their point of view (Sleep), how you seem to them and what their life experience has created in them. Remember that everyone has Many I's, and try and Separate the offensive I's from other things you know about this person. Remember that you are offended where you are most Identified and that the source of the inner account is within you (your requirements).

***

QUESTION:

What would other forms of identification be called?

RESPONSE:

Negativity, feelings of superiority, having Pictures and Imagination about yourself, holding accounts against others, Fear, greed and all the other Wrong Work of Features. Vanity is especially Identified.

RESPONSE:

Imagination is separate from identification, yes?

RESPONSE:

Yes, these are two different functions, BUT Imagination is present in Identification and vice versa.

4
PERSONALITY

A person developed in the Work -- to the degree that they are relatively free from the power of False personality -- can interact with life and people with a clearer perspective on reality. The obstructions of inner considering, mechanical momentum, features and identification lose power as True Personality evolves.

* * *

Not reacting from personality, negativity, identification is key to moving forward. You must be willing to be patient and to make humble efforts. Results will come. Moments of sudden illumination will occur.

***

QUESTION:

Would attitude be associated with consciousness?

RESPONSE:

No. Attitudes are acquired Personality traits. They are never Conscious.

QUESTION:

As one's consciousness expands, would there be a change in one's attitude?

RESPONSE:

Of course. As your consciousness expands, your perspective
expands, your Understanding deepens, your Knowledge grows,
your Being develops, and almost every attitude you now have
ceases to exist in the light of Consciousness. The Work creates
this kind of change. Sometimes in a moment. More often with long
intentional Work. Be sure that any change in attitude remains
consistent with the Work and the change will become permanent.

* * *

If you are working from False Personality, you will feel
satisfaction. If you are really doing the Work, you will feel
humility. False Personality is tenacious and will resist,
kicking and screaming all the way to oblivion. It is very cunning
and it will protect its interests. You can challenge, if you are
unsure, any I in order to discover its authenticity. Does the I you
Observe represent what is Real in you? If you ask yourself
this question when you have this doubt, the answer will be clear to
you.

* * *

QUESTION:

I was at an oppressive seminar today and took Collin to read.
There was a passage on the "extinction of personality" which
jumped out at me. I realized the enormity of what was being said.
this is not a grafting of some interesting ideas onto a false
personality, but a complete "extinction". Now this is a very
frightening thing and I think it may reflect where I am right now.
an enormous struggle that is profound in its implications.
and it does make me afraid.

RESPONSE:

Recognize that not everything that belongs to Personality is trash
to be discarded. Surely you have experienced sincere compassion
or real forgiveness. The reason Self-Observation needs to be

uncritical, which means not Identified with what it Observes, is so you can see everything objectively. It is only from that perspective that you can discern true and valuable from false and worthless. Last week, I gave you an illustration of how you can eventually turn a negative activity into something positive and creative without dismissing the activity. This kind of adjusting to the right attitude is as much a part of reconstruction as discarding is. The Work asks you to "Know thyself", then you can choose to Become. But first comes Knowing everything that is in you from a point of view that can make value judgments and has the force of the Work to carry them out. Does your fear relate to not knowing what happens after the "extinction" of Personality? Or is it being in that space where False Personality has perished before True Personality has been formed?

Acting may be necessary at times for some. In which case, it should be Intentional and as true to authentic Being and Objective Conscience as you can get. Other than these should be rare occasions, the Work asks you to make that False Personality passive whenever you can. If you give yourself permission to be asleep in it, so that it can function effectively, you are not on the right track. The Work requires of you that you eliminate bit by bit the False Personality that you Observe. If you find yourself in awkward stages, reflect upon the value this Work has for you, and continue in silence. It is essential that you Work to be rid of Wrong Work, not just Observe it.

***

As we have all verified, it is impossible at first to not feel revulsion with one's False Personality. This is where the Work becomes very subtle. It is also a paradox. One must Observe, discern, and Separate from all forms of Wrong Work, which consists of Negativity. The feeling of revulsion in relation to what is false and impure in you has relative validity and can contribute to the force you seek for change. This revulsion, however, once again is the Wrong Work of the Emotional Center. Revulsion is also a Negative Emotion. The Work will proceed with more alacrity if Inner Separation and Non-Identification take the place of revulsion. This approach to dealing with seeing False Personality will contribute to a permanent change.

***

Ouspensky said to Nicoll "Why are you sad?" Nicoll said "I didn't realize that I was." O. said: "It is a habit with you". Recognize that disgruntled-ness has unmet requirements. Recognize habitual emotional states. It is correct that you cannot not be False Personality when you are in it. You can however still Observe it. When you do, make it be quiet.

The silence is the space where Observing can happen. The power to stop False Personality grows there. A slight amendment -- Making False Personality quiet involves the effort of stopping its manifestations. Whether this is successful or not, a degree of inner quiet is a choice I believe you can make now.

***

QUESTION:

I can sometimes curtail outer manifestations of False Personality but I can still feel it inwardly. Is there a difference, from a Work point of view, between inner manifestations of False Personality and external expressions? What is the specific quality of 'making Personality passive'?

RESPONSE:

Yes, there is a difference between inner and outer expressions of False Personality. But the Work teaches you to Observe and Separate from both. It is the quality of "detachment" that defines making Personality passive. It is the exercise of not responding to any I that comes from False Personality, having no emotional response to it.

***

QUESTION:

I have observed many times over that observing makes me more quiet. But I have also noticed of late an ability to ease up on myself a bit. And actually enjoy myself.

RESPONSE:

This is good to hear. Talking is often just the automatic expression of False Personality. Observing it makes you want to be more quiet, less noise from False Personality. This gives you the opportunity to be more real.

QUESTION:

True personality requires me to talk a bit, yes?

RESPONSE:

Yes, True Personality talks quite easily without Inner Considering. But it doesn't require you to talk, life does.

***

QUESTION:

This is connected with the distinction between the "active" me whose I's are in operation with the psychological absorption attending them, and the Observing I that must passively and helplessly watch on. I have made some efforts along these lines and have found that it is useful in some cases to allow the I's to continue expressing themselves and elicit Observing I in a passive mode, even having a helpless feeling with it. Notice, express the "I", and watch. The immediate urge to somehow change the "I" seems to me to be False Personalities attempt to clean up what you are observing. This way False Personality thinks it has improved matters and one can now stop observing because everything is better now. This can muddy real observation.

RESPONSE:

This is a subtle and important perception. It is very common to find False Personality trying to imitate what it believes is a Work personality for anyone's benefit, including your own.

***

Real I seeks to exert control over Personality in order to be authentic, in order to replace Wrong Work with Right Work. As False Personality is observed and studied and worked against, it loses power, refuses to function, and eventually dissolves, vanishes to be replaced by your True Self, awakened, intentional, internally free, authentic, unique, purified of the labyrinth of Wrong Work, self-interest, and the Negative Emotions connected to them.

Real I is connected to Higher Consciousness, Objective Conscience. It has perfect integrity and contains the meaning and fulfillment of your existence.

***

Observe how Personality doesn't want to change, doesn't want to make any efforts, especially ones that eliminate its existence.

So this is part of Necessary Suffering, that is, sacrificing False Personality, which is always painful in some way in order to gain a real Self that is more truly you and in which there is no pretense.

***

Work I's oppose what you have always known as "yourself" but they come from you, they are in you, and even dormant they are more You than any imitation or pretense. The aim in the Work is to change. Is this your aim? Then you must change your "cherished sense of yourself". If you want to DO the Work, then you must continue to practice. Be passive to the resistance of False Personality. Expect it and just observe.

***

Once false personality has been observed, it ceases to function smoothly or at all. Sometimes we are left without the faculties to interact with the world. This state is part of the evolution in the Work and it can feel like "psychological vertigo" but it is temporary.

***

You are describing the experience of feeling the loss of your personality. It feels like "psychological vertigo". That sense of panic comes from not knowing who you are without your personality.

You will notice that the "frightening feeling" vanished once you were again firmly entrenched in personality through your exchange with the colleague.

These experiences reveal that there is nothing behind false personality, nothing to stand on. Your house is "built on sand." And nothing authentic as been created to replace it yet (true personality). This is a common experience in the early stages of Work practice. It comes from shining the light of consciousness on personality.

Ouspensky himself had the following experience early in his practice of the Fourth Way: in a letter to a friend, he stated that he did not know who would be writing the next letter (which I) and this frightened him. Seeing our multiplicity and disconnecting with our former sense of self is very unsettling. But we need to realize that "I am not that" and that this is a temporary transition.

***

We are hearing from some of you about the "psychological vertigo" accompanying this process which begins with the deconstruction of our false personality. This vertigo is being expressed in a sense of panic, a feeling of emptiness, a feeling of fear or anxiety, or sometimes the sense of being a fraud. The best way to deal with it is to try to practice inner separation in relation to those feelings and realize that this is a natural, temporary response in the process of the Work. The way to eliminate that negative experience is by building something real internally which will act consciously in the world. The way to build that in yourself begins with and relies upon self-observation.

When the mind is filled with the constant babble of inner considering and the heart is motivated by the self-interest of inner considering, the potential of receptivity to a higher state is lost. That is why all practical Work is focused on self-change or self-transcendence. The possibility of intentional, psychological self-generated evolution lies in this process of purification. The means is self- observation.

***

Remember that the aim of the Work is psycho-transformation.

***

There are many positive elements that can exist in False Personality. They are, however, still mechanical, still asleep, and though they may be more pleasant to deal with, they are no less false than any other aspect of acquired personality. They can work against you and your aims to develop in very insidious ways. Someone who is mechanically positive with a pleasant personality will have a harder time finding a reason to change or see anything wrong with their behavior in the first place. They will lack motivation to change.

* * *

When false personality I's try to observe themselves, they are enamored with what they see.

***

This confused state, although powerful, is temporary and a common experience in the beginning of the Work. The uncertainty, the loss of identity, and the terror that these feelings create is the "psychological vertigo" that accompanies the state of recognizing False Personality with an undeveloped observing I.

***

There are so many opportunities to see False Personality, Vanity or Pride and everything else the Work tells us to observe in everyone's every day experience that it is nearly impossible to not notice them functioning...if you are observing.

To use an example: perhaps you are a rather witty fellow, intelligent, perceptive, with a keen sense of humor (perhaps a Jovial body type). In almost every social situation you have the wittiest remarks, you can top anyone's story, you can level your friends with one witty word and you enjoy this about yourself. Your friends enjoy it too. You perceive yourself to be a good- natured, humorous person.

This nice, funny guy is the false personality, but you cannot see it when you are only being it. Everything about the false personality emanates from self-serving motives. Inner considering, which makes up most of the false personality, is obsessed with "what do others think of me", "do they see me?", "can they tell that I'm special?", "am I being treated properly?", "have I been insulted?", "have I received the merit and recognition I deserve", "am I attractive enough?", "are my clothes 'right'", "am I making the impression I wish to project?", "do I have what I want?", "do I have approval, acceptance?", "am I being foolish?"...

All of these thoughts and emotions belong to false personality . One can see vanity in them, one can see pride, one can see insincerity and dishonesty, and eventually one can see the complete mechanicalness of it all.

When one verifies what one knows to be the truth of the Work regarding oneself, the recognition creates a separation (some space for non-identification). Observing and verifying mechanics creates a powerful force that doesn't want to be mechanical. If that force is strong enough, it can create permanent change. More often, force will be accumulated over a long period of observing the same I's behaving the same way regardless of observation.

Any self-justification in this process should be considered a red light that inner considering is at work and that you must not listen to it. So back to our witty fellow. Suppose he is trying to work on himself and so he has an aim to make his personality passive. What does that mean? It means that he chooses not to go with his mechanical reactions in life. Perhaps the next time he is with a group of people, talking, laughing, with personality flowing abundantly, he will recognize his desire to make a funny remark as arising from the need to have attention, to be appreciated and recognized as the wonderful fellow that he is.

His Work effort then would be to remain silent. And in doing so, for the first time, much that he has missed can become clear. Because he is not projecting his personality, he can be perceiving reality in a different way. He may see some poor other mechanical person caught in the momentum that he was able to resist.

He may see fear or pain where he never would have noticed before because his attention was consumed with himself. He may recognize that his contribution, had he made it, was basically irrelevant and had no other purpose than to gratify his vanity. And if he can see this one little piece, then perhaps he can begin to realize that it is the same with all the other little pieces. Consequently, his real importance in the world has nothing to do with whatever his personality has to offer it, but what he has to offer the world without his personality in the way.

***

QUESTION:

I have made a profession out of personality, the raconteur, the improvisational conversationalist, ..and the transparency of One "I" to the Watcher means I can't fool myself. It may be Fun but it isn't

Work. And there are heaps of these guys.... so the question is to do with attitude to the racket being exposed.

RESPONSE:

Everyone comes into the Work with their personality, whatever type it is, in full force. It is a condition sleeping humanity lives in. The work of self-observation, which is foundation in the process, requires intentional effort. Included in this intentionality is the practice of being uncritical about what one observes. If your observing I responds with hating what it sees, then that is where you will be stuck, in a constant war between the observer and the observed.

The whole point of self-observation is to give one an objective view of what one is really like. Without objectivity, you are not going to see anything.

Keep observing I passive. That effort is part of making the effort to observe.

When you have the psychological space that objectivity requires, you have a toe-hold on inner separation. Then you can observe personality in all of its manifestations. This type of self-observation after a long period of time will show you much about yourself.

The aim of the Work is to transform the acquired, automatic behavior into enlightened, intentional action. In this process, the ego (false personality) made up of only self-interest, must be displaced gradually with a more evolved self. Purifying the emotional center, purifying the psychology of self-interest, is the substance of the Work.

I suggest that everyone "in the Work" reflect upon their motives for making these efforts. If one's motives have something to do with gaining personal power, that self-interest will effectively block any kind of real development.

***

You have made an interesting observation in seeing that you "sacrifice yourself in order to appear natural to others". This is indeed the case and can be easily verified by all who observe themselves honestly. False personality betrays essence when it seeks approval, pretends to be interested in things it is not in order to "fit in", or the thousand and one ways it lies out of inner considering.

The tragedy of false personality is that it does sacrifice our deeper selves, smothers our essence, and defeats our Work aims for the sake of being accepted by others. This is a high price to pay and almost everyone around us pays it for a lifetime.

* * *

QUESTION:

Although false personality is still a speeding freight train which can not be stopped at times, this is a most surreal experience, to observe false personality and watch in horror as it continues on. Could it be possible that I sense an almost mocking attitude.

RESPONSE:

Absolutely. It is necessary to know organically (from experience) the strength of false personality and therefore see the condition of sleep. That of humanity and that of oneself. But what is "It" in you that "sees"? Contemplate this question. It will help define and strengthen that part of you.

***

QUESTION:

I observe that lately I have withdrawn from friends and family to some degree. I find that it is with those that I am most familiar that I lapse into the deepest mechanical behavior. How does one develop a proper outlet for social behavior if one falls asleep when so doing? I have no impulse to "talk" to them about the Work.

RESPONSE:

When you find that your existing personality cannot handle a social situation, make the effort to make your personality passive. Just observe.

***

QUESTION:

Nicoll observes in his Commentaries that "You cannot change if you stay the way you are". He describes self-observation as the cornerstone for these efforts. My question, which may appear a bit pedantic, is this: how can you know when you are "uncritically" observing yourself, whether or not you are still peering through a filter of false personality? How does one verify that one travels in a sure and proper direction, and not further into the abyss of sleep and self delusion. Somewhere I read either in Plato or Aristotle a similar conundrum: how can one learn anything new when one has not yet developed the faculty for recognizing it? Sometimes I wonder whether we live in little Alcatraz's of our own, dreaming of escape and fantasizing that we are observing ourselves. Is this why O. says escape is impossible if attempted alone?

RESPONSE:

False personality judges, criticizes, justifies, feels offended, gets angry, has likes and dislikes, attitudes, opinions, feels ashamed and insecure.

When you practice self-observation, if you find any of these elements in the Observing I then you are identified with what you are observing. That is a trap that leads to insanity.

Observing I MUST be made objective, uncritical of what is being observed, yet seeing it clearly for what it is.

Think of observing as taking photos, registering, passively seeing.

What can you observe objectively about being irritable? Is it an unpleasant feeling or do you picture yourself as a "lovable grouch"? (There is no such thing, by the way). Are there any I's that secretly enjoy the zing of negative energy? What I's are irritable? The ones that want something that they don't have, the ones that have to do something that they don't want to do, the ones that are feeling inadequate, unsatisfied, unsure? We could go on and on, but the point is that all of the above and more belong to inner considering, to acquired attitudes, likes and dislikes, etc. That is ALL that the Work tells us that we must separate from.

Knowing this can give you the force to become detached and in that state of non-identification see clearly what intentional right action is. Then you lose all motivations and justifications for being irritable.

So, how do you know if you are observing yourself through a filter of false personality? If Observing I is objective, non-identified, then false personality CANNOT be present. One must work at this also, making Observing I not react with identification. This is difficult work as well, but it leads to liberation, to that escape from the prison of sleep that we seek.

Ouspensky was right about needing help. We need the help of knowing a way out and the help of someone who knows also that "way" from experience and can assist you through the difficulties and help you avoid the traps. Someone who really knows the way can help you to verify for yourself the ideas of the Work and their transformative power.

To be absolutely sure that your work is progressing in the proper direction is easy. Follow goodness. Seek to act with un-self-interested intentionality. Every normally formed human being has the innate knowledge (faculty of recognition) of what GOODNESS is. The Truth in it resounds in your soul with recognition.

***

Earnest efforts will gradually create a stronger Real I in you.

If you can recognize that your negative states are caused by the requirements you have (of the world, of people, of your life) in order to feel satisfied, then you will know that these requirements are based in false personality and inner considering.

We Work against these by making personality passive, by inner separation, by non-identification, by recognizing that inner considering is only self-interest, by sacrificing your need to be gratified.

***

Be patient while Working. Results are usually a long time in coming, but growth is every step of the way.

Observe identification. See the strength of the grip that it has on you. See the same grip it has on others. See how it fills you with energy, how you get a little thrill from the jolt of it. See how it is full of justification. See that the agenda that fires your identification is self-serving and so is the next person's, and the next, though the identifications may oppose one another.

This is where to make personality passive. The "why" is so that you can see through the false personality and all its obstructions to a higher level of scale and relativity which can free you from identification.

***

Essence is the innate nature you are born with. Whether you are active or passive, positive or negative type, or whether you are predisposed to being centered in the intellectual center, the emotional center, or the moving-instinctive center all belong to Essence with which you are born. You can verify this by observing the striking differences in types among very young infants and children.

This essence, which is your nature, then interacts with the external circumstances and events of your life's experience to form a "personality". Example: an active/negative type born in a large family may easily develop a loud, hyperactive personality in order to compete for the attention it desires. Then the influences of culture, family attitudes, opinions and behavior are all imitated or rejected automatically.

Clearly there are an infinite number of combinations of essence and experience which produce the unique individuals who are nevertheless all stimulus-response organisms.

This is a natural and necessary developmental process of acquiring a personality that can interact with the world and events. However, from the Work point of view, this acquired personality is created on the basis of self-interested need that originates in brain stem urges for self-preservation. So the acquired personality is called False Personality in the Work because it has been created through environmental influences and self-interest as opposed to enlightened or objective knowledge. It is mechanical, functions on automatic, and is asleep.

The process of awakening in the Work leads to True Personality. Through the process of self-observation, inner separation, non-identification, we learn to see that our automatic behavior does not reflect our true Self. The efforts undertaken reveal to us the malformation of our psychology. The accumulated I's of observation gain strength enough eventually so that one may act intentionally rather than mechanically. This intentionality issues from True Personality. It is not based on self-interest, but rather on objective consciousness. Long-term self-observation will strip away or melt away or burn away the wrong work of False Personality bit by bit.

Although the process is painful, to be rid of unnecessary suffering and have the clarity of mind and strength of will to act intentionally is liberation from the chains of mechanicalness that bind us in sleep. Psychological freedom brings new life expressed in True Personality.

True Personality still contains essence, types and different centers of gravity. But they are all at the service of higher consciousness. This means that you are more honestly yourself than you can ever achieve through any avenue of False personality.

A person developed in the Work -- to the degree that they are relatively free from the power of False personality -- can interact with life and people with a clearer perspective on reality. The obstructions of inner considering, mechanical momentum, feature and identification lose power as True Personality evolves.

***

What you are seeing when you experience yourself as "simply a bundle of tape recordings and reactions responding from these" is False Personality. It is relevant because it makes up your present reality. You do have a True Self which doing the Work will lead you to discover. The process of discovery begins with relentless practice of self-observation. It is imperative that one is uncritical of what is observed.

You are not only programs and mechanics. There is something in you that is authentic, unique behind all of these things. That Real I, True Self begins to gain strength or surface with the first observation of False Personality. Since you know already that there is something in you that isn't only mechanical, the I that knows this is the I of self-observation. That I is the beginning of who you are (Real I). And although at some level we are all one, we are also each completely unique.

Once you have observed in yourself (verified) that Sleep and Mechanicalness and False Personality exist not only in you but also in everyone else, it becomes easier to forgive BECAUSE you understand the nature and the power of Sleep. This helps to reinforce Real I which will then give you more power to forgive and understand.

***

Understand that the desire to be seen, noticed, have importance, be accepted, feel appreciated, are all natural strivings that arise from the brain stem urges that seek the security and connectedness of social relationships. So these emotions are not only a natural function of the human personality, but they are the same in everyone, regardless of whether the person has developed a personality that manifests those urges differently.

***

QUESTION:

Then there is the issue of compensation- in order to compensate for what may be a fear of being invisible or a belief I refuse to see that I am invisible- I exaggerate. I must excel at everything. In the past, as a much younger man, I dressed lavishly. At a younger age, I weight lifted. As a student in University, I wrote essays that stood out by covering a subject as completely as possible, often three or four times the required length. Today, I have my own office in the most prime location possible. Of course, it is never enough and deep down there is often a sense that I am 'faking it' that I am an 'impostor' . All this is from a deep need to be 'seen', to 'matter'. To be invisible is a painful, humiliating experience.

RESPONSE:

Of course it is never enough, partly because gratification-seeking has no end, and partly because this sense you have of "faking it" or "being an impostor" comes from a deeper level than the world can satisfy. This deep need you have to be "seen", to "matter" is only painful or humiliating if you believe it is. In reality, it is unnecessary suffering and you can simply let it go with the recognition that you do not want Vanity governing your life and actions.

There is a paradox here. This deep need to "matter" can be strictly vanities (emptiness) or it can be, even at the same time, the force behind the effort to find meaning. Finding real meaning in your life makes all the small I's of self-interest fade into nothingness.

The next time you find yourself feeling these emotions make an exercise to turn your psychology around 180 degrees and concern yourself with everyone else's welfare, anyone else's needs. If you are not tangled up in Inner Considering, you may notice that someone else is in need or that everyone else is full of Inner Considering as well. They are adjusting their clothes, worrying about their breath, smoothing down their hair, flirting and showing off, bragging, telling jokes, being vulgar, or anything else to get attention. The difference is that they cannot see this. You have seen and so you have made the first step in the possibility of self-transformation. Seeing is the first step to change if you are willing to.

***

If you are with a group of people and you are all operating fully in False Personality, then each of you has self-interest as motivation for your personal agenda which forms requirements of this event. You each want to be appreciated, behind your empathic interest with the others may even be the intent of being seen as amiable and as a good person or a compassionate friend. You're worried if you still have garlic on your breath from lunch. You're resenting some one's inattentiveness or perceived insult. You want to make your point. You want your point to be heard, understood, and validated by everyone so that you know that you're right and so that they know that you are right. You're flirting with someone who is married and you are insulted when they don't flirt back. You wonder what's wrong with them. Then you wonder what is wrong with you. Then you wonder if you are talking too much, or if you really like these people after all. And on and on. There is no useful exchange of energy in this kind of situation. It is all automatic, mechanical, predictable, and pointless.

However, let's say you are with your group of people and you are not in False Personality, which is made up mostly of Inner Considering, what might be going on with you in these circumstances? Might you not be able to see the condition of sleep, the flow of mechanicalness, the predictable stimulus-response behavior, how negativity is contagious, how it most often runs the show, how one association leads to another, how people use buffers, what pictures they have of themselves, what issues they are dealing with, what level their being is, what their features are, what their suffering is about?

If you are in External Considering, seeing from this point of view will evoke compassion for everyone's wrong work, and forgiveness. You could soothe the insecurity of one, absorb passively the negativity of another, include the excluded ones, and generally respond with conscious intentional words and actions appropriate to the circumstances. I hope you agree that this would be a better place to be in. If you do, then imagine your meeting with these people if they were also all Externally Considering. You can freely give to them your attention and care, and they give you back the attention and care that you need which will be an entirely different kind of need than that which comes from False Personality. That is an appropriate exchange of energies between people, each Externally Considering the other. Now imagine the whole world like that, everyone Externally Considering everyone else all through their lives. No fear, no hate, no taking only giving and receiving -- that would be purpose enough, don't you think, to do your own part in it, to be one more person on that side of Consciousness.

***

QUESTION:

How can I instill in myself a preference for Work I's that have all the appearance of being the interlopers in my being?

RESPONSE:

First know that they are not "interlopers". Work I's oppose what you have always known as "yourself" but they come from you, they are in you, and even dormant they are more You than any imitation or pretence. The aim in the Work is to change. Is this your aim? Then you must change your "cherished sense of yourself". If you want to DO the Work, then you must continue to practice. Be passive to the resistance of False Personality. Expect it and just observe. Observe how Personality doesn't want to change, doesn't want to make any efforts, especially ones that eliminate its existence.

Through the long process of Self- Observation, Work I's accumulate. You will gain a sense of authentic Self (versus imitation and pretense) gradually.

So this is part of Necessary Suffering, that is, sacrificing False Personality, which is always painful in some way in order to gain a real Self that is more truly you and in which there is no pretense.

***

QUESTION:

It seems insulting to ego to submit to this observing and separation.

RESPONSE:

Observing I exists although dormant throughout the adult life of every person. Each person has momentary glimpses of that higher perspective. In the Work, we make the effort to observe and separate for the purpose of growing. It is more than insulting to the ego, it is the end of its tyranny.

***

QUESTION:

How do we effect the shift in attention from the False Personality to the Observing "I"?

RESPONSE:

Begin by trying to notice or even just sense your state. Note also that Observing I is elusive in the beginning and in effectual however, with practice and patience Observing I gains presence and grows in relation to real efforts.

***

QUESTION:

It (this state) is utterly useless and of no real value!

RESPONSE:

That's why you're in the Work. Being mechanical has no meaning and it always leaves you feeling empty.

QUESTION:

Sorry...not really a question there. Just a realization of the futility of filling oneself with momentary and transitory 'excitements'.

RESPONSE:

False Personality and the I's of Inner Considering can never be satisfied. These aspects always need more attention, more gratification. Notice that when you have requirements, let's say of another person, and that person gives you what you want at the moment, the next moment you want more or something else. These transient I's associate without discretion and keep your attention and momentum on automatic. We must always return to the work of Self-Observation. It's the hard labor of brick laying.

But it builds something.

***

QUESTION: On a couple of occasions I have been able to interact normally while observing myself. At other times, I cannot do this and fall silent.

RESPONSE:

That silence, though awkward, contains the possibility of not acting mechanically. If you are confused in this silence, let go of the requirements you have that are creating confusion. Practice Inner Stop and accept the silence.

QUESTION:

But the silence makes others uncomfortable. I do not wish to appear self-absorbed. Is this wish not external consideration in some degree?

RESPONSE:

Possibly, it may be External Considering. But I would say that this is an unavoidable experience in the early stages of the Work. Other people will find that you are behaving differently. They may or may not be comfortable with that. That is their problem. Yours is to be able to interact in a sincere way without experiencing the absence of Personality. I'm sorry but this takes practice like any other achievement. It is something you have to work at and in the beginning it is awkward and confusing and out of pace with the flow of False Personality around you.

***

QUESTION:

Tearing down what is false without taking care to build what is genuine seems to court disaster.

RESPONSE:

It is not courting, it is creating disaster. The process of tearing down what is false should happen gradually along with the growth of Understanding which should take the place of what was false and is no longer a part of you. But it's like reining in a wild team of horses. Everyone wants results and particular results and right away. All seem to need external, tangible evidence that this Work is actually working. It is important to study different aspects of these transformational ideas. At the same time, trying to apply them to a psychology in the chaos of wrong work won't have healthy results. I reiterate and ask you all to continue the fundamental practice of Self-Observation with PATIENCE. You have each had some experiences of raised consciousness or deep insight. Let these inspire you to work without requirements knowing that you will receive what you particularly need in order to proceed.

***

The bucking of False Personality is to be expected, probably with bursts of negative energy. Here in itself is a set of I's. These I's don't want to make the effort to do the Work. These I's don't want to see, don't want to change, and aren't sure where they're going. You have another set of I's. I have a stack of papers from you writing about the Work in extensive detail. This belongs to another set of I's. You have I's that get negative, then discouraged, then desperate and wind up confused and lost. And you have I's that have a great deal of Understanding and intuition for Truth.

***

Observing I will be able to see everything clearly in time. It may be years before you can have a satisfactory effect on observed behavior. But what you are seeing is not only Vanity. It is also imitation, Inner Considering, and False Personality. These things diminish under the light of Self-Observation and a more conscious action takes their place.

***

QUESTION:

I can see imitation in others far more clearly than in myself. I see them make silly faces or grimaces which they probably think demonstrates to others some wonderful quality (though I wonder what I do that I cannot see as well). It all appears to be 'affectation' and completely unnecessary. I would like to see it more in myself and less in others.

RESPONSE:

What you are observing is False Personality and you are probably seeing more falsehood in it than ever before. Keep trying to see yourself objectively. Practice at observation creates a better quality of Observation.

QUESTION:

Why is there the automatic reaction of irritation when seeing falsehood in myself or others?

RESPONSE:

Falsehood is impossible to deal with psychologically. There is no ground beneath it. It is uncomfortable and frustrating.

***

QUESTION:

So you say that false personality is the result of wrong work of the emotional center?

RESPONSE:

Not exactly. False Personality is what you have acquired since birth and it is based on the wrong work of the Emotional Center.

***

QUESTION:

This is connected with the distinction between the "active" ME whose I's are in operation with the psychological absorption attending them, and the Observing I that must passively and helplessly watch on. I have made some efforts along these lines and have found that it is useful in some cases to allow the I's to continue expressing themselves and elicit Observing I in a passive mode, even having a helpless feeling with it. Notice, express the "I", and watch. The immediate urge to somehow change the "I" seems to me to be False Personalities attempt to clean up what you are observing. This way False Personality thinks it has improved matters and one can now stop observing because everything is better now. This can muddy real observation.

RESPONSE:

This is a subtle and important perception. It is very common to find False Personality trying to imitate what it believes is a Work personality for anyone's benefit, including your own. I am so glad that you continued reading about Internal and External Considering. This area of study in the Work is profoundly enlightening and gives you a good sense of where you are going.

***

QUESTION:

I saw myself today. And I saw a buffer quickly interceding to protect an apparent inner contradiction. While on the telephone, I made a comment that was out of alignment with my Work demeanor; in fact, it was a clear mis-statement. I had said that "I had complained" about something the other day when this was not really the case -- I had actually only brought attention to the subject out of concern. My statement was called into question by my friend and I had to admit that I did not mean to say that I had "complained" about it at all. I was only being flippant and unnecessarily severe in my comment.

At this moment, I saw myself. I could see that I was operating from a set of I's associated with my friend on the telephone and not the I's that I often operate from when alone or with someone else. These were clearly a separate set of I's and the sudden observation of them was jarring. Also, at this moment, I felt the imposition of a buffer whose intent was to protect me from this observation. I was able to refuse the buffer and alter the set of I's. I felt the need to physically change my posture, sit down, and operate from more sober and less flippant Work-related I's. My tone of voice changed and I began to express myself in a more sincere and genuine way through the rest of the phone call. After the phone call, I found myself struggling to keep this impression before my mind, wishing to keep this observation vivid. By doing this, I could see better what artificiality in myself means and I could then see new I's coming in to follow up behind the earlier ones and quietly take me on to the next state.

RESPONSE:

You caught a glimpse also of False Personality which is what generated the exaggeration. That you were able to pull yourself up out of the momentum of False Personality and the I's particularly related to this person required intentional effort. I'm sure you consider it worth it. To be functioning rightly according to Work knowledge at any time is a real foundational movement of your psychology in the right direction.

***

QUESTION:

I don't understand. I seem to have a problem accepting feelings in terms of my "psychology." They are from a different part than "thinking," aren't they?

RESPONSE:

Yes. But your psychology is not your thinking process. It's the makeup of your whole psyche. When I ask you to define your feelings then, try speaking in terms that describe the Emotional Center's experience.

* * *

QUESTION:

You mean you want me to tell you what the feeling was? to name it?

RESPONSE:

Yes. Is this insecurity, is it Vanity, is it Identification, is it Fear, etc? This is what I mean, what feeling generates the Inner Considering.

* * *

QUESTION:

It's insecurity, and fear - vanity is a way to cover it up, I think.

RESPONSE:

Now try to define where the insecurity comes from, and is it a valid state or an habitual attitude?

* * *

QUESTION:

Is it correct to say that essence has the potential to surface among friends?

RESPONSE:

Essence is more easily accessed or activated in a comfortable, non-threatening, informal situation "among friends". But it can surface anywhere.

QUESTION:

Should I look for this "quality" or "taste" of Essence or set this aside for now and focus on pacifying Personality?

RESPONSE:

It wouldn't be particularly productive to focus on Essence right now. Essence evolves as False Personality falls away. It makes its own expression known without you having to dig for it. Making Personality passive is one of the most helpful things you can do at this point.

QUESTION:

Will this render me cheerless?

RESPONSE:

I hope not. There is a stage in the Work that can last a long time when silence and retreat and reflection are most important. This has a definite effect on your Personality and it may seem flat, especially to others who know you . It is not that you are "rendered cheerless", it's just that you are changing and becoming more serious during this stage. What emerges gradually is authentic joy, from Essence, expressed in True Personality.

***

QUESTION:

My personality, as I look back over time has a pronounced acerbic wit, a sarcasm intended by me, and seen by me, as being funny. In attempting to make personality passive I note a pronounced decrease in the clever rejoinder, etc. It is such a pronounced difference that people see it quite clearly and my kids think I am nicer (because I have quit talking and listen). I also note when with a group of people, they are always interrupting and jockeying for position to talk, impress, etc. It almost is getting a bit strange and I lose my easy bearings in the midst of it. I am a bit confused, part of the vertigo thing.

RESPONSE:

Even if you are confused, don't imagine that you are lost. This condition is a natural side effect of the Work. You have witnessed others' sleeping Personalities butting against each other and have seen it for the impostor that it is. You are beginning to verify that you are not like that and do not want to be like that. To deal with "losing your bearings" strive for Inner Silence, Stillness. Be passive and don't Inner Consider behaving differently. This "vertigo thing" can be difficult to deal with but it is temporary. It only needs more time to develop Real I that can function naturally and independently in any situation. One more thing -- There is a place for humor and wit in Real I, True Personality, Essence. But not sarcasm if it hurts anyone.

***

If you look carefully, the "attitude" you refer to is not an honest I. Do you truly believe that you are more intelligent than everyone else in the world? You couldn't be intelligent and hold that thought to have any value. This "attitude" is perhaps just another aspect of False Personality that is acting in you to interfere with your Work efforts. We all have some of this kind of resistance in us. If you could suspend this "attitude" for a time, perhaps we can work through it to a different stage of development.

***

QUESTION:

Not all I's are from False Personality.

RESPONSE:

That is correct. Not all I's are from False Personality. That is why we have to Observe and identify them in order to Separate from what is false and nurture what is genuine.

***

QUESTION:

For a time now I have been unusually quiet, working in my yard, changing some patterns. My question. I seem on occasions as we have discussed to have suffered some confusion. Where am I?

RESPONSE:

I don't understand your reference to suffering some confusion. About what?

QUESTION:

Sometimes I sort of lose my bearing, get a bit morose.

RESPONSE:

What is "suffering some confusion"?

QUESTION:

A recurrent pattern of 'I's don't have clear vision of where I am headed and how I am changing. that is as well as I can describe it. It has been tough.

RESPONSE:

This "quiet" that you refer to has revealed the truth of many Work ideas to you. Has it not? In this quiet, you cease to be the artificial created Personality that you had no choice in creating. It's like stepping back away from yourself and your life and seeing it all with new eyes. Then you can hear and you can see and you can verify the Work. Eventually, you will choose from the position of Real I how your Personality manifests and it will suit you. This process may be taking place in the quiet space that may seem like emptiness now. There are real difficulties at this stage that have to be dealt with, however. Not knowing where you are headed or how you are changing is an experience you share with Ouspensky who wrote to a friend that he didn't know "who" would be writing the next letter. And this is one of the primary difficulties in the Work. You have to do the Work in order to receive its force and consequently verification.

Unfortunately, most often you have to do the Work for extended periods without receiving any results. Therefore, you get stuck at a point where your normal False Personality cannot function and you have no solid Real I or True Personality to replace it. Becoming quiet at this point is a natural response to this dilemma.

QUESTION:

I have noticed that my automatic Householder side has been impacted. I can see that this passage is not easy and fraught with danger. I could very easily see how someone could lose his mind, though I have no severe concerns in this regard. I can just see it.

RESPONSE:

First, what do you mean by "my automatic Householder side..."? How? I mean how has it been impacted?

QUESTION:

Taking care of my business in due course. Feeling a sense of surreality.

RESPONSE:

You are having an experience, like others here. You can assume this is a byproduct of doing the Work. This is a good thing in one sense. But you are right this passage is not easy and it is fraught with danger. Insanity is for the person who sees clearly what he is externally and has nothing internally that is more authentic and therefore more solid. The Work is meant to progress gradually, replacing the dying False Personality with Understanding and more intentional choices in action.

QUESTION:

I see gradual as to be preferred.

RESPONSE:

Be very sure that you understand what you are doing in the Work. The intention is to eliminate the False Personality and create a New Man based on Higher Consciousness. That means that you will necessarily have to undergo a complete change in your Personality.

QUESTION:

I am beginning to understand.

RESPONSE:

If you remain at a point of confusion, let's sort out the questions. The unsure footing, the psychological vertigo, the non-functioning Personality, the retreat into silence, are predictable results of progressions in the Work. This silence has been very helpful as well as disconcerting because in it you have verified many ideas and observed in yourself and in others these verifications. You have begun to change. Try again to release anxiety and other Negative Emotions. Try to be patient, you have already noticed a cumulative effect. This will increase. The definition you seek will take shape with your continued efforts. Please talk to me specifically about any dangerous areas you encounter. If you find no relief for this distress, call on me. Don't let it continue indefinitely without positive change.

***

QUESTION:

Through Observation I believe I can see various aspects of my psychology. How then can I more aggressively confront my psychology? --that is, how can I bring more pressure to bear to expose difficulties and overcome them? Should I Work more aggressively? -- or just take opportunities as they arise?

RESPONSE:

Take the opportunities as they arise. You will recall Nicoll saying that you cannot Work
in an Identified way, anxious and trying to force results. I don't want you to aggressively confront your psychology. I want you to passively Observe it and try to define what is Real I in it and what is acquired Personality and inauthentic to your Being. The most aggressive you should be with yourself is in repressing False Personality and making it passive. This is the beginning of Inner Separation which is the long, hard Work of cleansing the Emotional Center. Are you having any problems with a particular idea, such as knowing that your psychology is a separate entity from your physical body. Your present psychology which is mostly made up of False Personality is full of the attitudes and opinions, likes and dislikes, and multiple I's that you have acquired. These I's that you have observed verify for you that your Personality is full of them. They need to be made passive so that the Work can be active.

***

Nicoll: "The second education that the Work consists in is about observing the psychology that everyone so easily takes for granted, a definite makeup, from which they can gradually become free if they practice self-observation in the light of this teaching. Has everyone verified that the Many I's of False Personality can eventually lose power and you can become free of the False Personality and its tyranny?"

***

QUESTION:

One aspect that is difficult to deal with is that False Personality arises when it chooses to. It fills me up with attitudes and opinions and talk. It is like the "See 'n Say" pull-string toy. What's more, when this happens, I feel that I am 'that', that is, I take 'that' to be me. I cannot decide to not be False Personality. At times I can operate from Work I's but this is weak and momentary. I also observe an attitude of disgruntled-ness that I bring to many situations. This is somewhat like the comment that Gurdjieff gave to Nicoll when he said, "Nicoll, you go around with a pocketful of stones, ready to throw at people." (Nicoll, "Informal Work Talks and Teachings", 51)

RESPONSE:

Ouspensky said to Nicoll "Why are you sad?" Nicoll said "I didn't realize that I was." O. said: "It is a habit with you". Recognize that disgruntled-ness has unmet requirements. Recognize habitual emotional states. It is correct that you cannot, not be False Personality when you are in it. You can however still Observe it. When you do, make it be quiet.

QUESTION:

Quiet, not stopped.

RESPONSE:

This is correct. The silence is the space where Observing can happen. The power to stop False Personality grows there. A slight amendment -- Making False Personality quiet involves the effort of stopping its manifestations. There comes a time when your distaste for False Personality is so strong that you will begin to want to make choices that weaken it.

***

QUESTION:

I can sometimes curtail outer manifestations of False Personality but I can still feel it inwardly. Is there a difference, from a Work point of view, between inner manifestations of False Personality and external expressions? What is the specific quality of 'making Personality passive'?

RESPONSE:

Yes, there is a difference between inner and outer expressions of False Personality. But the Work teaches you to Observe and Separate from both. It is the quality of "detachment" that defines making Personality passive. It is the exercise of not responding to any I that comes from False Personality, having no emotional attachment to it.

QUESTION:

Detachment -- meaning "this that I am observing is not me"?

RESPONSE:

It is more than this. It is knowing what this Being is, not just what it isn't.

***

QUESTION:

I seem to be noticing an alarm going if I slip into a poor state. I note that I am slipping into some low grade angst type state, for instance, and almost always as I try to justify the feeling there is something that says "there you go again" and so I give it the inner silence/stop exercise. immediately the FALSE PERSONALITY starts to quibble with the new view of things. but I stick with it, observe, and the grip is loosened a little. I also note some sensations that go with this process in the area of the solar plexus.

RESPONSE:

What does False Personality have to say when it quibbles? Can you describe the sensations in your solar plexus?

QUESTION:

OK, let me try to describe. I am so used to going with a depressive feeling as being totally warranted under the circumstances. I know I learned this, principally from parents and these I's are convinced they are right to give in to the feeling, very entrenched. The new feeling in the solar plexus is difficult to describe. it is almost like butterflies in the stomach but a little higher. like almost a feeling of fear at the approach of this new ability to quell the negativity, something totally new and almost frightening. But it is happening consistently, that is, the refusal to go with the low grade I's and the funny feeling of newness and almost a lack of bearings. It is hard to describe.

RESPONSE:

Well, you did a good job anyway. This is a perfectly natural experience in the Work. That you are able to Observe and even prevent the expression of old Negative I's is an accomplishment even if you are inconsistent at it. But you have said it yourself: These very strong Identifications are convinced they are right and are firmly entrenched. That is the definition of Identification. It is consequently understandable that when you usurp an entrenched characteristic it leaves a vacuum and something that you felt very attached to disappears, leaving you with that feeling of no bearings. If you continue to practice as you have been, you will get to a point where you are so free from old Identifications and

Pictures and Imagination about yourself that there will be no False Personality to quibble with. You can be and if you continue earnestly as you have been, you will be free of all of the Wrong Work that stands between where you are now and your full potential.

***

QUESTION:

Does the artifice of False Personality ever become to seem like a ridiculous burden? Like baggage and "drag" released? As if what we have tried to protect all these years was what made us feel so bad and sick at heart? This is what I imagine it to be.

RESPONSE:

False Personality is both ridiculous and seriously suffocating. I don't believe we try to protect it. It protects itself. I think that at least people with Magnetic Center want to be free of artifice. And it does turn out to be the False Personality that is "sick at heart" and makes us feel bad. Does this make sense to you?

QUESTION:

Yes, the idea that we are not the False personality that connives against us.

***

QUESTION:

In other Commentaries Nicoll also speaks of "hating the enemy" (False Personality)

RESPONSE:

As we have all verified, it is impossible at first to not feel revulsion with one's False Personality. This is where the Work becomes very subtle. It is also a paradox. One must Observe, discern, and Separate from all forms of Wrong Work, which consists of Negativity. The feeling of revulsion in relation to what is false and impure in you has relative validity and can contribute to the force you seek for change. This revulsion, however, once again is the Wrong Work of the Emotional Center. Revulsion is also a Negative Emotion. The Work will proceed with more alacrity if Inner Separation and Non-Identification take the place of revulsion. This approach to dealing with seeing False Personality will contribute to a permanent change.

***

QUESTION:

Can I see too much of myself? -- or is this not possible?

RESPONSE:

It is possible to see too much of yourself, that is your False Personality, if you have not enough Real I present to give you centeredness or stability. Other than that, holistically speaking in terms of the Work, it will be necessary for you to see everything that you call "myself".

***

QUESTION:

Today, I recalled an experience I had with my grandfather as a child. It brought up the same feeling I had at that time, which was sadness.

RESPONSE:

This is not exceptional since Personality traits are imitated in families. Your mother's sadness may be an imitation of her father's sadness. Overall, sadness is self-absorption and lacks Scale and

Relativity. It is also Negativity which is the Wrong Work of the Emotional Center. The next time you Observe yourself feeling sad, first, say to yourself "this is automatic behavior". It is Negativity which the Work asks us to not express. Remember that it is imitation and try to Separate from the habitual and familiar taste of it.

***

QUESTION:

I am trying to interpret Gospel stories in the light of the Work.

RESPONSE:

You will be fascinated and enlightened by Maurice Nicoll's "The New Man" and "The Mark" if you are trying to make connections with the Work.

QUESTION:

The Work brings life to the Gospels for me.

RESPONSE:

That is what it is meant to do.

QUESTION:

When the Christ said, "It is not I that doeth the work, but the Father within me, He doeth the work. Was he not referring to the Real I?

RESPONSE:

He was referring to that individual part of your true Self (Real I) that is in touch with "the Father".

QUESTION:

When he said, I of myself (false personality) can do nothing, wasn't he recognizing his nothingness that the Work proclaims we should do?

RESPONSE:

This is correct. Recognizing not only his nothingness, but the inability of False Personality to DO.

***

You experienced a group of I's that make up a Picture you have of yourself in False Personality. This is acquired Personality and it is Real I that had the experience "who on earth was I talking about?". Real I knows that the "who" you were talking about is not Real I. Therefore, it feels "odd".

QUESTION:

The closest I can describe it was I was almost embarrassed to talk about these I's that belong to False Personality and was a bit sheepish about it. Anything but authoritative.

RESPONSE:

So, Buried Conscience awakens and challenges False Personality.

***

QUESTION:

We are in false personality, having no Real I to guide. My question relates to the vantage we take to assure that we are not lying and making it just grow.

RESPONSE:

This is one of the biggest pitfalls in the Work. Many people use the Work ideas to reinforce their False Personality instead of disassembling it. One of the ways to discern whether or not you are "lying" is to ask yourself whether you are experiencing any ego gratification from your Work activity. If what you are seeing and saying in your Observations pacifies you, then you are in False Personality.

QUESTION:

What is the False Personality's greatest weapon or group of weapons?

RESPONSE:

False Personality's strongest weapon is Identification. Fight it with detachment.

***

QUESTION:

How does one assure that one is being completely Sincere about these efforts, and not a pawn of False Personality?

RESPONSE:

Can you not tell the difference between the taste of truth and the taste of lies? I think you can. Are you trying to?

QUESTION:

Yes, I am trying to and I think I can tell most of the time but the interests of False Personality are very powerful and cunning, I think. I have had a few small tastes of the freedom non-identification affords, and I can see false Personality shifting, or attempting to shift the valuable lessons in its interests.

RESPONSE:

If you are working from False Personality, you will feel satisfaction. If you are really doing the Work, you will feel humility. False Personality is tenacious and will resist, kicking and screaming all the way to oblivion. False Personality may even be responsible for the kind of "plagues" that others have experienced recently. It is very cunning and it will protect its interests. You can challenge, if you are unsure, any I in order to discover its authenticity. Does the I you Observe represent what is Real in you? If you ask yourself this question when you have this doubt, the answer will be clear to you.

QUESTION:

It is just that sometimes it is like a house of mirrors.

RESPONSE:

That is exactly what seeing Multiplicity is like. And the False Personality consists only of Multiplicity. Remember that Nicoll says that recognizing one's Multiplicity is a definite stage in the Work. It shows real progress. You can find the image that is Real I by destroying the false images in you.

***

Nicoll writes- "For a very long time we mix the Work with our associations, with the machine of personality, which is driven by life and reacts to it mechanically. And this is inevitable because only a gradual separation is possible. A person cannot be torn suddenly away from personality. It would destroy him. So even though we try to work, we identify with the reactions of personality which seems more distinct and real, or more 'natural'."

***

What you will find is that even when your real motive is unselfish (posting a question to help another student), the Negative I's that belong to False Personality's pictures, pride, fear, vanity will raise their heads and each make its own remark. Remember that these are only the I's of False Personality. They aren't truly YOU. Though they may be familiar thoughts, that doesn't mean that they are valid. The old habitual I's that taunt you and challenge your Work are just old I's. They are the things you always say, without actually meaning them. For instance, when Timothy McVeigh was convicted, I remember saying something like "Well, I'm glad I won't have to go there and kill him myself". This I came from self-righteousness and old False Personality behavior. Would I kill him really? I would forgive him. I didn't mean one word that those I's said. Nevertheless, they were spoken. Challenge any I that challenges your Work. If it is not true, dismiss it.

***

QUESTION:

I believe that Nicoll says in the Commentaries that there is no psychology in the false personality. Am I correct there?

RESPONSE:

Yes. In the Work, psychology is something that you develop. Before you develop it, you are only a stimulus-response organism according to the Work.

***

QUESTION:

Yes. I can see that more and more. I saw my father, a very methodical man, with everything in place, taking his bath just on Saturday night, etc...but I see certain things in myself that are like that. When I do see it, I change quickly because I don't want to be like my father.

RESPONSE:

Much of our Negativity is based on the unconscious imitation of our parents. This is why Personality is called "acquired". It is not our true Self.

***

QUESTION:

When contemplating conquering Personality, I think of the phrase, "Are you prepared to die?" Is there any validity to this viewpoint?

RESPONSE:

It is precisely apropos. However, ONLY when taken metaphorically. This is not a simplistic matter of semantics which is why I make a point of it. Religious language is dangerous to people who do not understand the esoteric meaning. Of course you know that this "death" has to do only with the False Personality.

***

QUESTION:

As I have tried to observe myself, I seem to find fear as the root cause. It seems to generate identification, formatory thinking, false personality, and on and on. I don't know if this is true or if it's my own current dark state of mind. I would appreciate your comments.

RESPONSE:

You have seen clearly into the source of many aspects of the Wrong Work in a person's psychology. But Fear is at the source of Identification, etc. We fear rejection, being alone, being in need, being vulnerable. We are afraid of failure, commitment, appearing to not fit in, looking foolish, and deep inside more than anything we fear meaninglessness.

QUESTION:

Meaninglessness. Yes, this fear seems to be the basis of my personality. Without my image of myself there is nothing.

RESPONSE:

All of these fears are Negative Emotions meaning Wrong Work of the Emotional Center and they result in Wrong Work in Personality. You are mistaken, however, behind the image of yourself is your true Self. A related quote from Thomas Merton. "Even when I try to please God, I tend to please my own ambition, His enemy. There can be imperfection even in the ardent love of great perfection, even in the desire of virtue, of sanctity. Even the desire of contemplation can be impure, when we forget that true contemplation means the complete destruction of all selfishness -- the most pure poverty and cleanliness of heart." The result of doing the Work correctly is Humility. Make sure that this is what you want. Your Fear of meaninglessness can be force for Work.

***

We are dealing now with strictly internal matters. I was referring to being passive in yourself to yourself. If you are in this state, you are not in False Personality and you will not respond to others from that place. When I said that you don't need to be passive to others in this exercise, that is because this exercise is not about others. Being passive to other people's Personalities is a different exercise for a different purpose. One more note on making the Personality passive. If you are a passive type Personality, then becoming passive to your Personality may require you to become active.

***

RESPONSE:

If over achieving is a repeated scenario in your life experience, it may be necessary that you STOP trying....

QUESTION: I see what you mean. Yes surrender has not been easy for me.

RESPONSE:

Surrender can be understood as another word for Non-Identification or acceptance. Non-Identification can pull the rug out from under Personality's momentum.

***

QUESTION:

Could you say something about resistance please.

RESPONSE:

Your Personality will resist the Work. It doesn't want to make the effort, but more importantly, it is protecting its existence. I know this seems strange, but it is rather like something in you desperately trying to hold together the Multiplicity to avoid the loss of ego. Sometimes, you may experience only a slight struggle. Sometimes you have to beat the bear.

***

In reference to Humility, there is an aspect of fearing the unknown, but I believe the resistance against it has more to do with being afraid of being vulnerable. Humility feels very much like vulnerability. The truth is that they are opposites. Humility frees you from all the insecurities of False Personality.

***

QUESTION:

It seems that unnecessary suffering and negative emotion overlap a great deal, if not totally coextensively. All of it boils into a bad state, which is most unpleasant, useless and wasteful. It has helped me to realize I am more like a baboon than Mozart when I indulge all of it.

RESPONSE:

Unnecessary Suffering is always Negative Emotions and Negative Emotions are always Unnecessary Suffering. And all of it belongs to False Personality Every kind of suffering that comes from unsatisfied Personality is what has to be sacrificed in order to make room for purified emotions. When you can trace some bit of Unnecessary Suffering to something that happened in seventh grade and has stayed in your Personality ever since, there is powerful liberation.

***

The object of the Work is to make Personality weak which is a disadvantage at first. Every time you go against Personality consciously, you gain and are stronger. Personality is acquired. You contact and experience life through your Personality. You do not see your Personality directly. It is not conscious to you. Your Personality renders life to you according to ITS shape. Personality is: HABITS of mind, emotions, behavior. It is necessary to study the Personality; what your apparatus is like.

If you do not Work on Personality, we remain mechanical. Even seeing Personality you will not be able to alter anything, at least for a long time (that doesn't mean don't try). Personality is a machine that controls you. Personality grips you and you fall asleep in its grip and so behave in the same ways. Once you are in Personality everything happens mechanically, automatically. You do not see it. When you awaken a little, you see the machine to which you are attached. You feel imprisoned, even afraid of the manifestations of Personality and afraid of your inability to control it. This Personality was created (acquired) without your knowledge or consent (mechanically). Work on yourself means Work on Personality. The Fourth Way is "in life". You cannot go into a monastery or sit in a cave to free yourself from Personality.

 Making Personality passive is continual Work on yourself. The means (tools) are Self-Observation, Inner Separation, and Non-Identification. You must take mental photos of yourself over a long period of time. This will reveal that your usual conception of yourself is very far from Reality. In this Work, you must learn to know the real from the invented. Later, to separate them. A person must realize that they indeed consist of two sides, observing and observed. As long as you take yourself as one person, you will never move from where you are.

 Observing I is passive and Personality is active. When you understand your powerlessness over Personality, your attitude changes -- to caring about becoming
Real. You understand that you are not your Personality. It is a mask, a part you play. Sincerity will show you that you are under the power of Personality and at the same time you feel that you are not only Personality. You begin to fear Personality and question everything because whatever you would do or say is done for you by Personality. The Aim at this level of Self-Observation is to be free of Personality.

***

The idea of Humility is abhorrent to the ego, False Personality. And in the English language cultures it sounds far too much like humiliation, which is completely unacceptable to the vain False Personality.

***

You have perceived deep levels of motivation and functioning in your acquired Personality. What you have Identified as "fear of survival" is present in everyone in varying degrees. It belongs to the primary instinctive drive (brain stem urge) in every human, which is self-preservation. If your Instinctive Center was threatened with starvation in infancy, this experience would most likely create Fear, frustration, panic about being powerless, distrust of the world, insecurities about your ability to get what you need. In infants powerful feelings about self are laid down in acquired Personality closely connected to Essence feelings which are active at the time. This further empowers these "concepts" you have about yourself because they are buried so deep and feel so much like you to yourself. This will give you some idea of the very real power that acquired Personality has. It would be from these fears and insecurities that the idea (Picture of yourself) of being "inept" arose.

This idea is actually a feeling you have about yourself and is where you are Identified with yourself. Your particular Identifications would probably seek to be in control either of situations or yourself and possess power which feels far more secure than being vulnerable. Any perceived threat to these features of acquired Personality would be felt as a threat to your very existence. This dynamic is the same in everyone's psychology. Each person's experience forms their idea of themselves around Essence which is present at birth.

This happens to everyone and is necessary. In the Work it is called the First Education. It is unavoidably based on instinctive self-interest and necessarily so. This idea of who you are is not a reality. The thoughts and feelings ("I's") that belong to it were acquired through individual experience. If your experience had been different, your feeling of I would be different. However, it would have some other acquired feeling of I, also based on experience interacting with Essence. The Personality that is formed in this way cannot afford to have its sense of self jeopardized or shaken because what is behind it is weakness, i.e. fear, insecurity, shame. It wouldn't do to have others see you as weak.

That would undermine the False Personality and reinforce fear and insecurity. The feeling you have of being "inept" is one of the many emotions that belong to Internal Considering. Internal Considering is a branch of Identification. It is full of I's that care most of all about how others see you and treat you. It (Inner Considering) worries about the impression you make, the notice, understanding, interest, appreciation, etc. that you receive. Inner Considering cares about position, merit, power, status, wealth, beauty, health, possessions, and more.

All Inner Considering is the Wrong Work of your psychology. Long Work on understanding these specific ideas plus Observing and Separating from acquired Personality are some of the intentional efforts that will result in freedom from this Wrong Work and its consequences. If you know that your feeling of being "inept" was laid down in your psychology without your consent when you had no options, and was intensified by being connected directly to Instinctive-Centered Fear, then exaggerated later on by Vanity, Pride, etc., you have an Objective view that can loosen the grip of acquired Personality enough for you to realize that it is NOT YOU. Real I, true Self, is buried under the mountain of acquired Personality. Gradually getting rid of your Wrong Work will reveal Real I and empower it.

Your Essence experience of humiliation only underscored the relationship between Inner Considering and Instinctive deprivation and Fear. Vanity has also played a big role in forming Inner Considering in you. The simple point in all of this is realizing that no matter where your own personal Wrong Work began, you can be free of it since it does not express your most authentic Being. All of your psychology is based on self-interest unless and until you develop enough Consciousness and Being to become selfless in your motives.

This Work develops Consciousness and Being and you can see how Humility (the absence of self-interest, no Inner Considering, no Wrong Work of any kind) is a necessary factor in the process. I regret having to Verify for you that sleeping humanity does function primarily from the Moving-Instinctive level of Being. There are different levels in all centers and the Moving-Instinctive level is the lowest in each, the path of least resistance. The most automatic and mechanical, stimulus-response functioning belongs to this level. There are also higher levels in each center and in each person. The Work tries to get us to live in these higher parts of centers where we can receive higher influences that lead us toward increasing development of Consciousness and Being. It is indeed a paralyzing thought to realize that sleeping human beings, whose nature is beneath that of animals, are the blind leading the blind into constant chaos.

It takes very little observation to Verify this. To say that the human species is different from other organic life-forms and valuable only in terms of potential is a deep Work idea, actually Objective Truth. And while, without development, there is little difference between an animal and a human being, the difference is extremely significant. After all, animals don't make wars, they don't kill for pleasure or gain, and they are never malicious, greedy, or deliberately cruel. While human beings are destroying the planet and all of their own species through these exact activities which are beneath the animal level of existence. We each ought to at least raise our level of Being above that of Fido.

***

Recognizing the "taste" of Negativity is a critical development in the Work. This cognizance will inform you, long before your mental processes can, of the nature of an "I" or state. Developing further a distinct Dislike for that taste will assist you in Separating. The slums of your psychology refers to the lowest level of being within you. Not everything (I's) that resides there is strictly False Personality. Recognize higher levels of Being in yourself as well and direct your attention there. This will aid in discernment. Fear is a very difficult Feature to deal with. The Instinctive element has legitimate Fear I's that are very hard to be Objective to.

Fear also hides and expresses even more fear when it is Observed. It will paralyze you and keep you stuck where you are. It tends to infect every thought and greatly exaggerates Internal Considering. To Work against it whenever you recognize it working in you, Separate from it and examine it to the extent that you can. Real legitimate feelings of Fear exist to inform us that there is danger. However, you can have this exact same "feeling" based solely on Identification. You can learn to discern which is which by taste (Instinctive Centered knowledge) and by questioning the I's that express Fear. Ask: What is this Fear about? What exactly am "I" afraid of? Does this Fear come from False Personality (Inner

Considering)? What are the I's from Fear saying? Are they honest? Do they express a Truth or only one narrow angle? If you can do nothing else, try to practice Inner Silence toward Fear I's that you have Observed before and know are not of real danger.

To practice Inner Silence, allow for the awareness of Fear I's in your consciousness WITHOUT giving them your attention. Do not talk to them or listen to them internally. Reach for that still, silent point in the center of the tumult. Remember that Features act automatically so question your first response when you recognize Fear, without closing your eyes to any information it might provide. IN GENERAL, don't trust this feeling of Fear. It is usually made only of Imagination, but it will ruin your entire life.

Another exercise you can use is: Every time you feel fear, let it become like a bell, a Reminding Factor to Stop and Separate. In addition, since this (Fear) is an emotion, you can purposefully direct your inner attention to Intellectual Work to keep your mind occupied and unavailable to Fear I's; read, write, plan, problem-solve, use Creative Imagination, etc. It is absolutely correct to say that that choice is to be made by an individual's awakened Conscience.

While awakened Conscience may produce the same level of Objective Morality in separate individuals, its inner direction (instruction) will be different in each person and each instance. Do not go against what you recognize as awakened Conscience in yourself. To Work towards the growth of Essence is not a matter of being able to lay your hands on it, metaphorically, and rouse it into activity. It is approached in a more indirect way through practicing External Considering and eliminating the False Personality, especially the Wrong Work of the Emotional Center. Try to suspend Fear so that Conscious Mind can function. Essence will EMERGE as the Work progresses in you. The dichotomy of experiencing the Work as miraculous and wonderful/disconcerting and frightening is a definite and common experience in the developmental process. Be patient here. You are definitely on the right track. The "inner connection" within you and that "still, silent point" are the same thing. It SEES and is NOT what it sees. Its

knowledge is Understanding and it is Real I in you. You
have experienced it as connectedness and through Non-
Identification in that silent place. Ask yourself: What is it in you
that has been Observing and Seeing so much?
Then try to discern the answer by inner touch and taste. This will
increase the presence
of that which Observes.

5
INNER CONSIDERING

QUESTION:

You have said that we should look for the I's that are creating states. I have made notes showing two columns. On one side I wrote down a state or mood I observe in myself. On the other side I wrote down what I consider to be the "I" behind this state... example: Resentment --> "I don't like being criticized". ...example: Joy --> "I like music" "I like singing"...example: Frustration --> "I don't like not getting answers"...? -- and what should I be looking for in this? It seems to come down to likes and dislikes.

RESPONSE:

It does come down to likes and dislikes which are part of acquired Personality and part attached to Essence. This all belongs to Inner Considering. Inner Considering is full of opinions and attitudes, likes and dislikes, needs and desires, and essentially everything you think of as yourself. This is why it is so difficult to separate from Inner Considering. These elements "seem" to be real because they are all you have ever known yourself to be. However, everything that belongs to Inner Considering is acquired, is self-interested, and will obstruct the process of the Work. The Work places a great deal of emphasis on studying all of the aspects of Inner Considering, which is the current state of your psychology, in order to eliminate the obstructions they create. Since all the aspects of Inner Considering are acquired, they are subjective and can change. That which belongs to Real I does not change. It is connected to Objective Conscience which is universal and unchanging.

***

Along with the "normal" wrong work of every machine, if you are dealing with Fear that could account for more emotional dysfunction and the feelings of being alone since Fear will not take emotional risks and therefore is cut off from authentic emotional relationship. It may also fuel your need for reassurance in order to feel comfortably yourself.

You are seeing a lot already. You have identified Vanity I's and laziness. The more you photograph them, the less you will want to suffer the pain and the wrong work they create.

You are very perceptive to notice the element of self-interest (seeking appreciation) in your complimenting of the guard. On closer examination, though, I think you will find that the I of self-interest was not the real I of motivation. I imagine you really were grateful and it was externally considerate to express that. The other I that felt self-important was probably only the automatic I of your own False Personality, an acquired habit of thinking of yourself in particular terms.

Work on Emotional Center first by refusing to identify with every Negative Emotion that appears in you.

* * *

All Inner Considering is the Wrong Work of your psychology. It is like always being in your own way. Long Work on understanding these specific ideas plus Observing and Separating from acquired Personality are some of the intentional efforts that will result in freedom from this Wrong Work and its consequences. You have an Objective view that can loosen the grip of acquired Personality enough to realize that it is NOT YOU. Real I, true Self, is buried under the mountain of acquired Personality. Gradually getting rid of your Wrong Work will reveal Real I and empower it.

The simple point in all of this is realizing that no matter where your own personal Wrong Work began, you can be free of it since it does not express your most authentic Being.

All of your psychology is based on self-interest unless and until you develop enough Consciousness and Being to become selfless in your motives. This Work develops Consciousness and Being and you can see how Humility (the absence of self-interest, no Inner Considering, no Wrong Work of any kind) is a necessary factor in the process.

***

If you are looking for causes ("what is it that causes us to begin to internally consider") the following quote provides some. Nicoll: "The answer is that what is at the bottom of it all is where you identify with yourself. All forms of internal considering, of which making accounts against another person is one form, belong to identifying. The Work says that we must study identifying down to its very roots. A man is only offended where he is identified with himself. And the Work also says that the study of identifying must begin with a study of where you are identified with yourself. It is here that you can be upset, hurt, offended, insulted, and so on. The being identified with oneself comes first, being upset and offended comes second, making inner accounts comes third."

***

Being concerned with other peoples' opinions is the essence of inner considering. Always worrying about how you are being "seen", "perceived", "treated", "understood", "appreciated", and "noticed" by others is a prison of self-interest. This is where everyone lives in their psychology. This is the natural state of waking sleep. Understand that the need to have attention, the fear of "invisibility" arise from the natural human instinct for self-preservation which includes social acceptance.

Those of us in the Work strive to be more than just the animal nature. So...

1. You cannot be exploited or used if your actions are intentional.

2. Trying to imagine what other people think is a complete waste of time and energy.

The need for attention and the fear of invisibility are probably more specifically connected to vanity which is part of inner considering. Vanity will go to absurd lengths to make sure that it is not invisible.

You need to practice inner separation in relation to all of the above. You cannot see clearly what you are only feeling.

* * *

QUESTION:

Nicoll says, "the study of identifying must begin with a study of where you are identified with yourself". When this "WHERE" is discovered, what is to be done with it?

RESPONSE:

When you discover "where", ask yourself why it exists there. In the light of the Work's answers to this question, practice Inner Separation. For example, if you are identified with being an intellectual, that is how you perceive yourself. If that sense of yourself is not validated by others' responses to you, its accuracy is undermined, the Picture is challenged. This creates Inner Considering, insecurity, resentment, etc. The creation of this Wrong Work that belongs to Identification should be enough motivation for you to begin to let go of this particular set of chains.

***

An exercise to apply regarding accounts. Try to Observe what accounts you have with one particular person. Reflect on why. Have they hurt you? How have they hurt you? Do you resent them? Why? Is their behavior annoying, insulting, aggravating, infuriating? What does their behavior have to do with you? They are asleep, mechanical, full of False Personality with NO options

about how they manifest. So WHY do you have accounts?. Because you have requirements. You need other people to satisfy your requirements or you become upset because you remain UN- gratified. You need others to support the Pictures you have of yourself, otherwise you feel invalid. You need others to Verify that you are indeed valuable because there is nothing in you yet that knows its own value and doesn't rely on others' opinions to Verify it.
WHAT DO THE OPINIONS OF SLEEPING, STIMULUS-RESPONSE ORGANISMS MEAN TO YOU?

***

The Work should give you enough valuation to not be completely under the power of Inner Considering. Don' t let it ruin your efforts. And don't let it rob you of what you have already verified.

Take one aspect of Inner Considering and focus your attention on it. Observe it, try to be passive to it, try to separate from it, and keep trying. One thing at a time. It leads incrementally to Real I.

You have to find the place in yourself that is free of all of the aspects of Inner Considering in order to get to the stage where you no longer seek or need external validation. I can't give that to you and neither can anyone else. It is a matter of your evolution in the Work which depends on continued Observation.

***

QUESTION:

I had noticed that revenge I's are often coupled with negative future imagination so that one undoes a wrong in ones imagination. What I found astonishing was that I could remember slights from decades ago which today mean nothing to me and get so worked up and identified that I begin to imagine revenge. This is incomprehensible to me. I could say much more about this topic as well since I have recently observed revenge I's in me. (ironically 'revenge' comes from the Latin 'vindicare' which means 'set free'!)

RESPONSE:

Revenge is an extreme form of account making which belongs to Inner Considering which belongs to Identification. This long stream of wrong work that begins with Negativity created by Inner Considering can lead all the way to violence. If revenge I's are abundant in you, this suggests a serious state of insecurity and no attention being given to making Negativity inactive in you.

QUESTION:

May I give an example of a strong revenge I in me because I do not see the inner considering? I would like your analysis of the example.

A store owner refused to give my property back and was very rude, condescending and concluding the telephone call with "deal with my lawyer" and promptly hung up on me. I did everything in my power to try to recover it. I became more and more agitated and could not rest until I "got back at him". I thought of nothing but how to hurt him back, and get revenge. Eventually I did by pulling strings and having him charged with criminal offences. This rectified the wrong and 'set me free" (root of revenge) and I could rest again. Although when I saw him in court, saw a real person attending court, I felt bad for him as well and had the charges withdrawn. Question-where is the wrong work and specifically where is the inner considering?

RESPONSE:

You did stumble upon a phenomenon. As long as the wrong work of your Emotional Center is in place you can return to any painful memory and become totally identified all over again even if it is now irrelevant. This is one of the reasons why we in the Work try not to give Negative Emotions our energy or identification. You can live in painful Negativity permanently if you choose to let your mind wander among the various difficulties in your past. Or you can start new NOW.

First of all, Ghandi said "An eye for an eye makes the whole world blind". I would not call this a situation caused by Inner Considering. Undoubtedly you were dealt with badly. This does not excuse nor permit your own bad behavior (wrong work). In this particular case, it was appropriate to do what was necessary to regain your possession if possible. The phrase "do what was necessary" does not include trumped up charges, pulling strings, and essentially scaring the man half to death. Did this really make you feel better? Even if the Latin root of revenge means "to be set free", that's just etymology and has nothing to do the Work, In the Work, we set someone free as well as ourselves by forgiving them. Forgiving can't happen in the presence of wrong work. They are antithetical. Negativity is always wrong work. Revenge is only self-perpetuated Negative Emotions. Should he retaliate, will you then not need to have revenge again?

There is no real freedom in revenge regardless of what your emotions feel. If Emotional Center was awake it would not be possible to act in a violent or negative way toward another person. This is our Aim. This is true freedom. If you felt freed by this response, from humiliation or self-torment, you have it backwards. You should feel genuine remorse at your own wrong work and at understanding that you caused another harm. If he caused you harm first, it doesn't matter. You are only concerned with your own wrong work and inner state, not his.

***

On Inner Considering, observe:

-- Justifying, always putting yourself in the right -- the need for attention -- the desire for appreciation -- worry about what others think of you -- feeling excited when you're a social success -- feeling disappointment if you are not -- thinking always how hard you have it -- feeling superior, feeling inferior -- being nervous -- resenting not getting the notice or valuation you want -- being insincere -- feeling rejected -- feeling insecure -- worry

***

Ironically, what is required in Work against Inner Considering is that you lose yourself. So through the efforts that you've made so far, you have verified the existence of Multiplicity, Sleep, an absence of Real I, and how difficult it is to keep your attention focused for any length of time on any pursuit. All this without the discipline of School or preparatory Work. I should think that would be enough motivation to send you seeking after Work knowledge voraciously.

External rules, external disciplines will not help you. This Work is purely inner, psychological, transformational Work. Even if you were in a School full of rules and disciplines, you would find the energy of Observation dissipates rapidly and that is a natural occurrence.

Recognizing Inner Considering becomes one of the easiest aspects to observe after you have studied and understood what constitutes Inner Considering. These states become glaringly obvious and are very easy to see, not rare, with the effort of Self-Observation.
If you observe Inner Considering, probably the most you can do and the best thing you can do is to make your personality passive. External Considering is a long way down the road of knowledge in this Work. But making your personality passive by not identifying with your Inner Considering has to be accomplished before you can get to true External Considering. Luck plays no part in this process. Knowledge comes first, effort and practice comes after knowledge, and the result can be the creation of Real I.
What you need to serve as Third Force or "reminding force" is a strong desire for change and a good deal more knowledge of the Fourth Way Work.

Understand that the desire to be noticed, have importance, be accepted, feel appreciated, are all natural strivings that arise from the brain stem urges that seek the security and connectedness of social relationships. So these emotions are not only a natural function of the human personality, but they are the same in everyone, regardless of whether the person has developed a personality that manifests those urges differently.

In this Work, we try to evolve beyond the brain stem urges governing our actions in the world and forming our psychology.

***

When in the presence of other people, let your effort be only to register what feelings you have (alienation, fear, insecurity, superiority, etc.). Try to make an effort to make your personality passive. This can help you see more clearly. Later reflection will reveal that the obstruction you are experiencing in social situations probably has a lot to do with all of the issues of inner considering. Knowing this, observing this, verifying this will free you from it.

***

When the mind is filled with the constant babble of inner considering and the heart is motivated by the self-interest of inner considering, the potential of receptivity to a higher state is lost. That is why all practical Work is focused on self-change or self-transcendence. The possibility of intentional, psychological self-generated evolution lies in this process of purification. The means is self-observation.

***

Remember that in the Work we are trying to move from internal considering to external considering where the good of others is placed ahead of our own.

***

In the natural progression of the Work, having created an effective Observing I, one begins to see all of the wrong work of Inner Considering. With long term observation, you begin to see that all of your actions in the world are motivated by self-interest, even the outwardly charitable ones are subconsciously, mechanically seeking merit, appreciation, rewards. When you begin to feel the insubstantiality and immaturity that comprise all of the aspects of Internal Considering and if your aim is development of Being, these manifestations begin to fall away. At that point, you can no longer walk into a room of people feeling insecure about yourself without being aware that such behavior is mechanical and based solely on Inner Considering. It will feel beneath you to be functioning psychologically at the level of Sleep, like everyone else in the room seeking self-gratification. The dissolution of those I's of Inner Considering raises you to another level of consciousness. It takes you out of the stream of social momentum and mechanicalness.

If you are with a group of people and you are all operating fully in False Personality, then each of you has self-interest as motivation for your personal agenda which forms requirements of this event. You each want to be appreciated, behind your empathic interest with the others may even be the intent of being seen as amiable and as a good person or a compassionate friend. You're worried if you still have garlic on your breath from lunch. You're resenting someone's inattentiveness or perceived insult. You want to make your point. You want your point to be heard, understood, and validated by everyone so that you know that you're right and so that they know that you are right. You're flirting with someone who is married and you are insulted when they don't flirt back. You wonder what's wrong with them. Then you wonder what is wrong with you.

Then you wonder if you are talking too much, or if you really like these people after all. And on and on. There is no useful exchange of energy in this kind of situation. It is all automatic, mechanical, predictable, and pointless.

However, let's say you are with your group of people and you are not in False Personality, which is made up mostly of Inner Considering, what might be going on with you in these circumstances? Might you not be able to see the condition of sleep, the flow of mechanicalness, the predictable stimulus-response behavior, how negativity is contagious, how it most often runs the show, how one association leads to another, how people use buffers, what pictures they have of themselves, what issues they are dealing with, what level their being is, what their features are, what their suffering is about?

***

The constant state of irritation that you experience comes strictly from inner considering, i.e. expecting the world to accommodate you, having the presupposition from vanity that you should have your way in all things. The wrong work of inner considering is filled with self-interested I's ("am I getting what I want? do others appreciate me enough? do they notice I'm special?")

Being concerned with other peoples' opinions is the essence of inner considering. Always worrying about how you are being "seen", "perceived", "treated", "understood", "appreciated", and "noticed" by others is a prison of self-interest. This is where everyone lives in their psychology. This is the natural state of waking sleep. Understand that the need to have attention, the fear of "invisibility" arise from the natural human instinct for self-preservation which includes social acceptance. Those of us in the Work strive to be more than just the animal nature. So...
1. You cannot be exploited or used if your actions are intentional.
2. Trying to imagine what other people think is a complete waste of time and energy.

***

The need for attention and the fear of invisibility are probably more specifically connected to vanity which is part of inner considering. Vanity will go to absurd lengths to make sure that it is not invisible.

***

Inner considering, which makes up most of the false personality, is obsessed with "what do others think of me", "do they see me?", "can they tell that I'm special?", "am I being treated properly?", "have I been insulted?", "have I received the merit and recognition I deserve", "am I attractive enough?", "are my clothes 'right'", "am I making the impression I wish to project?", "do I have what I want?", "do I have approval, acceptance?", "am I being foolish?"...

All of these thoughts and emotions belong to false personality . One can see vanity in them, one can see pride, one can see insincerity and dishonesty, and eventually one can see the complete mechanicalness of it all.

***

You have made an interesting observation in seeing that you "sacrifice yourself in order to appear natural to others". This is indeed the case and can be easily verified by all who observe themselves honestly. False personality betrays essence when it seeks approval, pretends to be interested in things it is not in order to "fit in", or the thousand and one ways it lies out of inner considering.

***

The sense of loss and disappointment that you experience has a cause. That cause comes from having requirements that the external world needs to fulfill in order for you to have the positive experience you wish for. These requirements belong to inner considering. They are about whether or not you get what you want, things go as you plan, people treat you as you wish, and overall whether you are satisfied with the "event".

Inner considering is the nature of a normally developed psychology. But in the Work we are asked to transcend all of the complicated emotional issues of self-interest for the transcendent clarity of being without requirements.

The first step in that process is to notice when inner considering occurs. Then look behind the emotion to find the motivation. Are you disappointed, angry, irritated, insulted, neglected, sad, self-pitying? Are you "singing your songs of woe"? Are you justifying all of the above negative states?

Getting the world to meet all your requirements is an impossibility, of course. And although most people never stop trying to force that to happen, simply being detached from inner considering alleviates all of that unnecessary suffering. In that state that has transcended inner considering, you will find yourself without requirements. Your state will not depend on what others do or say, what you have or don't have, get or don't get. Since gratification is no longer your goal, you will find yourself at peace, filled with acceptance.

This begins a long term study, but have you discovered any ways of dealing with "accounts"? Can you see how they are related to Imagination?. Nicoll: "All accounts of this kind, all feelings that you are owed by other people and that you owe nothing yourself, are of very great psychological consequence to the inner development of a man. A man in the Work can only grow through the forgiveness of others. That is, unless you cancel your debts, nothing in you can grow."

Can you see how forgiving others and not having requirements of them could completely change this condition in you?

If you forgive others to gain something for yourself, this is not real forgiveness. I don't think this is about semantics, but forgiveness isn't a tool.

***

QUESTION:

It seems that inner accounts represent ugly pathological qualities in us and that canceling debts and removing these accounts is a kind of purging of these dirty things in us rather than a pseudo-forgiveness that we magnanimously bestow on others for their benefit and for our own artificial relief. Are you saying that 'account-making' is not just about people, but about generating an inner 'ledger' with credits and debits regarding life in general?

RESPONSE:

Making accounts definitely has two aspects to it in this regard. On one hand, we make accounts against people who offend us. But the more subtle accounts and potentially more damaging are the ones we have about what we "deserve" in life. We can more easily write off someone who insults us than we can be released from the feeling that we ought to receive more from life. It is true that the only real way of overcoming Inner Considering is by canceling debts and removing accounts of these kinds, and this happens before real forgiveness is possible.

***

QUESTION:

I was wondering if the need for self-approval is inadequately replaced through seeking approval from others or even through imagination. if this could create lots of inner considering , account-making , etc. . Also , is the need to come to direct self- approval innate in the mind?

RESPONSE:

Getting approval from other people or through your Imagination would be inadequate to satisfy the Personality's need for approval. The Personality belonging to an un-awakened person cannot be satisfied by any amount of external validation or even reward. It is bottomless. Needing self-approval is a backwards approach to the Work. The Work will not make you feel this. Indeed, you will feel the opposite. If the Work is Working in you, you will start to feel your Nothingness. This opposes "self-approval". This gauntlet must be undergone. What emerges, if the Work has been applied rightly, will be a self that needs NO approval because it is purified.

***

Let's return for a moment to the subject of Inner Considering. Nicoll: "What is it that causes us to begin to internally consider? Let us ask the question: "At what point or where do you start making accounts?" You start when you feel you are not estimated aright, when you feel you are undervalued. The waiter does not come when called. The shop-assistant serves another person first. Perhaps people do not look at you enough in the street, or, let us say, pay sufficient attention in general. Or one person seems persistently to ignore you. Or perhaps you hear what someone said of you: that is nearly always unpleasant. There are a thousand and one possible examples, less, and more, serious. Small incidents upset us easily -- the waiter, the shop-assistant. These form short accounts and may eventually become a habit. But we have all sorts of long-standing accounts against others, some of them stored up in the past, unfortunately for ourselves. They all begin with this mysterious question of one's own valuation of oneself."

It is another paradox that our insecurities form outward presumptions of superiority. This paradox exists in "one's own valuation of oneself". Does anyone find this familiar?

***

QUESTION:

I see it now as a self-centered focus that is excited at the thought of being passed over. This is aggravated due to being a passive type. Being ignored or interrupted is a common experience and I rebel against this with an inner attitude that demands to be heard and respected.

RESPONSE:

Ask yourself if the reason you have for feeling offended is valid, honest, true? Is it realistic to expect attention from sleeping people? What does the Work have to say about the reasons for your Negative Emotions? And have you Verified that an "inner attitude that demands to be heard and respected" doesn't work? It doesn't get you heard or respected, only aggravated. This is only the activity of Vanity.

If you are looking for causes ("what is it that causes us to begin to internally consider") the following quote provides some. Nicoll: "The answer is that what is at the bottom of it all is where you identify with yourself. All forms of internal considering, of which making accounts against another person is one form, belong to identifying. The Work says that we must study identifying down to its very roots. A man is only offended where he is identified with himself. And the Work also says that the study of identifying must begin with a study of where you are identified with yourself. It is here that you can be upset, hurt, offended, insulted, and so on. The being identified with oneself comes first, being upset and offended comes second, making inner accounts comes third."

***

Nicoll: "Our object is to try to awaken, not to be so identified with everything, not to be slaves to useless negative states and blank minds and so on. If we continually make accounts against one another by privately despising, by wrong talking, by psychological murdering others and so on, all work on oneself is spoiled. "In the process of awakening from sleep, one thing hangs on another thing. One leg cannot get out of the bed. The whole of you must get out of the bed if you want to stand upright."

***

If you want to diffuse old accounts, begin with trying to see within yourself what Identifications initiated the account. In a general sense, the way to do this is to put yourself in the other person's place. See from their point of view (Sleep) , how you seem to them and what their life experience has created in them. Remember that everyone has Many I's, and try and Separate the offensive I's from other things you know about this person. Remember that you are offended where you are most Identified and that the source of the inner account is within you (your requirements).

***

Forgiveness is the ultimate remedy for holding accounts. The path to it is directly through the Work.

***

So you see that you can have accounts against people who "apparently" deserve it. Their behavior has caused harm. Remember that releasing accounts frees YOU. And remember the other person IS ASLEEP.

***

QUESTION:

I was finding it hard to see accounts I had made. About a week or so ago I observed myself becoming angry because someone had ignored me and I was starting to imagine what I would do if the situation were reversed. This kind of opened the door for me and I began to see the many, many accounts I was keeping. One of the deep rooted accounts was with my mother who has been dead over nine years. Tonight, while preparing myself for the meeting by reading over the commentaries I began to think of this account I have not been able to deal with and as I read I began to try to put myself in my mother's place. She was a demanding and stubborn woman. We were at odds for as long as I can remember. On her deathbed I took her hand, when my father was out of the room, and told her that I loved her and forgave her for everything and that all that mattered was our love for each other. That night she died. The love I felt was genuine, but the forgiveness was not real. Tonight for the first time I began to see myself as she must have saw me. I hated her stubbornness, but I was just as stubborn. I was demanding and unbending. I never once in the thirty years we had together ever gave a thought to what she might have been feeling. I was so arrogant that until today I thought that my forgiveness may have released her from her six month coma like state. It was so much easier to hate the things in her that I couldn't see in myself. Instead of trying to forgive her, I should have been begging for her forgiveness.

RESPONSE:

This is a real experience of Understanding. And this is where the Work can lead you. Realize that true Forgiveness is inherent in genuine Love. What you did for her and yourself on her deathbed was appropriate if incomplete. You can probably count on the fact that she would feel just as you have and would have begged your forgiveness if it was possible. You gave it to her unasked and your motive was pure. If the Forgiveness was not accomplished at that time, it does not matter except for what it has cost you since. Now forgive yourself.

***

QUESTION:

We each have our own little avenues of expressing Negative Emotions and Keeping Accounts which may simply be on a smaller scale. As long as we are in our present state of psychological captivity, we are at risk of the vilest violence. I find that Account-Making is linked to Negative Emotions. Negative Emotions can have us extending our mechanical, unthinking reactions into the future by resorting to Account-Making -- that is, by holding others accountable for our bad reactions, or our inability to understand. Expressing Negative Emotions is a form of self-indulgence and a surrender to immediate impulses and a constricted sense of injustice. Not expressing Negative Emotions can redirect one's attention inward and can have us focusing on what is what at the heart of getting in to this state of affairs. Without Self-Observation in these moments, we simply roll out the familiar and predictable course which leave us with no insights and others with the stale effects of our inner filth.

RESPONSE:

This is accurate. A sleeping psychology can begin at a point where one Negative I starts a train of associative Negative I's that has its own momentum and can lead all the way down to the lowest level in a person. Violence. Example: "I hate getting up in the morning. My job drives me crazy. It takes all my energy. I'm so exhausted. I just need some rest. I can't get any rest. I always have something to do!. I wish I could get away from all this pressure. But I never get a chance like that. I have to work and then work some more while some people can take off whenever they feel like it. Why can't I get a break? I've always been so overwhelmed with responsibilities. My life is so unfair. It makes me furious that my sister can travel when she wants to and I have to always be the one to be responsible. Well, I've had enough. I can't take it anymore. I have to have a break or I'll die. If I don't get a break, I'll lose my mind." This descent into Negativity CAN really lead a person to insanity, suicide, or murder. So the first I of Negativity is always the first moment of possible violence.

***

This is an example of keeping accounts. When we give more than we receive, we feel that we are owed. Unconditional Love desires reciprocation but does not depend on it. There is no 50 % - 50 % in relationships that work. The equation is each gives 100 % plus. You did the right thing in Externally Considering your wife. All that you gave to her, material and otherwise, was a sincere act of Love. It is in expecting equal reciprocation that you were disappointed. Being disappointed because someone does not have the same feelings that you do about anything is a lack of perspective. It presupposes that the other person ought to be in complete sync with you whenever you desire that. I would like you to consider the fact that your wife is overwhelmingly preoccupied with the most important and frightening event of her life. To have requirements of her at this time is an extra burden she probably can't bear. Fearing the loss of attention and being cared for is abnormal as the sunrise but try to not have expectations, requirements, and even suspend your needs temporarily. This is an exceptional time in both of your lives. The closer you are, the better you can work everything out.

6
INNER SILENCE

To begin with, and maybe most important, you cannot hear anything when you are speaking. Also, you may be investing your emotional life in your Intellectual Center.
This will not work. Try practicing short periods of inner silence repeatedly. As you learn Inner Separation and direct your attention more intentionally, you will find more spaces for inner silence. The momentum of talking will reinforce Identifications. It will also keep you from accurate Self-Observation.

***

QUESTION:

My personality, as I look back over time has a pronounced acerbic wit, a sarcasm intended by me, and seen by me, as being funny. In attempting to make personality passive I note a pronounced decrease in the clever rejoinder, etc. It is such a pronounced difference that people see it quite clearly and my kids think I am nicer (because I have quit talking and listen). I also note when with a group of people, they are always interrupting and jockeying for position to talk, impress, etc. It almost is getting a bit strange and I lose my easy bearings in the midst of it. I am a bit confused, part of the vertigo thing.

RESPONSE:

Even if you are confused, don't imagine that you are lost. This condition is a natural side effect of the Work. You have witnessed others' sleeping Personalities butting against each other and have seen it for the impostor that it is. You are beginning to verify that you are not like that and do not want to be like that. To deal with "losing your bearings" strive for Inner Silence, Stillness. Be passive and don't Inner Consider behaving differently. This "vertigo thing" can be difficult to deal with but it is temporary. It only needs more time to develop Real I that can function naturally and independently in any situation. One more thing -- There is a place for humor and wit in Real I, True Personality, Essence. But not sarcasm if it hurts anyone.

The important thing for you to do then is to seek some Inner Silence so that you can Hear. Try stepping back and just Observing or even just Sensing your Inner states. Don't strain trying to separate. Transforming happens as the result of practicing long-term Work. You can't force it. One more thing: It is okay to be adrift sometimes. If you remain receptive, your bearings will come to you.

***

I found a good description of Inner Silence that I'd like to share. It's from Volume 1, page 213 of the Commentaries. The title is "Self- Observation". There are new connections made. This is a small quote: "The practice and meaning of Inner Silence in the Work is like this; First, it must be about something quite distinct and definite; and second, it is like not touching it. That is, you cannot practice Inner Silence in a vague, general way, save perhaps as an experiment for a time. But you can practice it rigidly in regard to some distinct and definite thing, something you know and see quite clearly. What you are practicing Inner Silence about is already in the mind and you must be aware of it, but you must not "touch" it with your inner speech. Practice this in relation to selecting thoughts, Negative I's, complaining I's, sets of I's that create Negative states, not going with I's from False Personality and Wrong Work, Identifications. Try Working with only one definite thing at a time.

* * *

QUESTION

I find Nicoll's comment a bit vague and hard to understand. Does he mean "Don't wrestle with the state?" Don't talk to it?

RESPONSE:

Yes, that's the intent. Sometimes you have to wrestle. But it should be rarely. The point being made about Inner Silence is that in the Work it is practiced in reference to a specific thing. In other words, if you have a repeated Negative response to a particular person or recurring state or I's, you can use the practice of Inner Silence directed at those specific issues. Is that clearer? "don't talk to it" is correct.

QUESTION:

Yes. But I must ask follow up if I may? Say I have a time of day. In the morning when I worry. What he is saying is to observe this in silence and note the predominance of this pattern of Is at this time, right?

RESPONSE:

Yes, and...he is saying not to let your inner speech touch those I's. You are aware that they are there, but you refuse to have anything to do with them. In the case of worry I's, you must always remember that worry is Negative Imagination and it would be something specific like this that you would practice Inner Silence in relation to so that every time you noticed "worry", you turn away from it. Don't give it speech.

***

QUESTION:

How is inner silence "about something distinct"?

RESPONSE:

Say you have a particular attitude that is Wrong Work .For example, public speaking makes you nervous. The practice of Inner Silence in relation to this distinct Wrong Work is to not touch it with your inner speech even while you are aware of its presence. If you give it no voice, it is silent and loses force. Is that a clear example?

QUESTION:

I see, it means you must be 'silent', inwardly, about something specific, something that is too often present in the mind.

RESPONSE:

Yes, this is correct. The silence is always about something specific. It is not a general silence like emptiness of mind.

QUESTION:

I see. And are you saying that this and other Wrong Work atrophies out of disuse?

RESPONSE:

Wrong Work atrophies under the influence of the light of Self-Observation and through the denial of Identification with it .Other elements come into play like thought selection and Inner Separation but a good deal of power exists in the light of Observing I.

***

QUESTION:

Is inner silence an accompaniment to self-observation? They seem [like] the same thing almost.

RESPONSE:

Very often Self-Observation leads to a kind of Inner Silence but it is an entirely different kind than the intentional exercise of creating Inner Silence in relation to a specific issue. The kind you are referring to is more about False Personality evaporating in the light of Observation, leaving a lot of silence in place of its normal noise.

QUESTION:

Is inner silence a refusal to give voice to a particular set of recurring Is, such as sad ones, or is it silence in relation to it?

RESPONSE:

The refusal to give voice to recurring I's has to be an internal one as well as an external one.

QUESTION: Please give another example of Inner Silence. My problem, i.e., whether you refuse to empower the issue or just watch in silence. Internally, are you inside or outside of the issue. I know this sounds abstruse in the extreme.

RESPONSE:

This Work practice of Inner Silence is about refusing to empower the issue by giving it speech. You are not watching in silence because you are not giving "it" that much attention. Let's say you Observe a habit you have of always having to have the last word. Assuming your Work Aim is to eliminate this Wrong Work of False Personality, you are instructed to be aware of this characteristic and refuse to "think" about it. You refuse to talk about it in your mind, you are aware of its presence and you make a deliberate effort to not act in this way by not allowing yourself to formulate the words that express this aspect of your False Personality. Internally, you are outside of the issue. You know the issue is there and you do not touch it with your inner speech. Therefore, Silence exists.

QUESTION:

I see, so these are not the I's of Self-Observation but the actual
Wrong Work I's manifesting that we are trying to be silent to.

RESPONSE:

Yes, this is correct. The I's that are Wrong Work are what we
suppose to practice Inner Silence in relation to, not the I's of Self-
Observation.

***

QUESTION:

How do we determine what wrong "I's" are appropriate targets of
our inner silence technique?

RESPONSE:

Choose one that you recognize easily, that has verified
consequences of Wrong Work and make it one that you want to
change. Start with patterns of Wrong Work that give you distress.
For instance, if you are afraid of flying and you must take a trip,
you do not allow any inner talking in relation to your fears. That
may be large or small -- it is subjective. It would be best to start
with single issues, and smaller issues when you first begin this
practice. You will have more success and you will learn more
consequently. A better example might be a recognized negative
attitude toward a particular person. This attitude is full of Negative
I's against this person . The attitude says "I can't stand him,
he makes me sick, furious, exasperated; he is so stupid ...etc.".
These are the words your inner speech gives this attitude which is
Wrong Work that you want to eliminate. If you refuse to give your
words to this attitude, it has no expression. You are aware
that you have these feelings inside but you do not acknowledge
them, giving them no voice.

Even more simply, take one single Negative I that you experience frequently and practice Inner Silence. Choose one that is easily recognizable, i.e. I hate traffic, I am impatient with my children, cooking dinner makes me sick, my mother makes me angry, laundry work is the worst drudgery, I worry about money, etc. Choose your own personal I to practice with and as soon as you hear that I turn your thoughts away from it AND replace it with intentionally directed thinking. It can be helpful here if you have a prechosen subject so that your attention can have a definite place to go without confusion. For example, planning your dream-house, vacation, job -- anything. Whenever you choose to direct your attention, the Aim is to give NO WORDS to that one I. Even if you remain aware of its presence, you don't talk to it, you don't listen to it, you do not allow it expression.

* * *

QUESTION:

Is the idea of "Suggestion, Assent, and Captivity" relevant to introducing moments of Inner Silence? -- that is, breaking off gathering I's in the earliest "Suggestion" stages.

RESPONSE:

Absolutely. It is between Suggestion and Assent that you can practice Inner Silence and effectively deflect Captivity.

***

QUESTION:

Is Inner Silence different from thought selection?

RESPONSE:

Yes. Inner Stop is different. You practice Inner Stop in relation to any Wrong Work that you Observe. You simply STOP all manifestations and become quiet and passive. Thought Selection is about choosing which I's to go with. You don't stop, you switch tracks.

***

QUESTION:

Identification is something I can see better at the end of the day
when I look back over things. But I noticed myself in a
conversation recently where I so wanted not to be
identified and I just out of habit went there. I felt hurt, etc..

RESPONSE:

Non-Identification should not hurt. Just the opposite. It should
heal. When you can't Separate from a Negative Emotion, it needs
further scrutiny. Try to discern what the I's of Identification are
saying and determine whether they are true. If this escapes you at
the time, practice Inner Silence in relation to your Identification.
Do not listen to its I's. Do not speak to them. Do not acknowledge
them. Reflection will inform you later about what the Identification
was.

Treat it with the practice of Inner Silence. When you notice where
your I's are taking you, stop and refuse to go. Try to recognize the
bad state you are left in after a trip through the slums of your
psychology. Loss of energy is the least of it. Negativity is
contagious. If you hang around it long enough, you will become
infected with its poison. This is even more significant than loss of
energy because you will then spread it further.

Whenever you notice you are feeling Negative, FIRST, stop. Next,
practice Inner Silence toward the thoughts and words expressing
Negativity. Later, when the state has passed, reflect on what the
Negative Emotions were that you felt. Name them. What
were they saying to you? Are these I's familiar to you? (Habitual)
Are they truthful? Try to perceive the source of your Negative
Emotions. It is inside you, not outside you. DON'T JUSTIFY
YOURSELF. Observe what is behind your Negative responses.
Try to get a sense of the "taste" of it. Is it pain, fear, frustration?

About what?

Recognizing the "taste" of Negativity is a critical development in the Work. This cognizance will inform you, long before your mental processes can, of the nature of an "I" or state. Developing further a distinct Dislike for that taste will assist you in Separating. The slums of your psychology refers to the lowest level of being within you. Not everything (I's) that resides there is strictly False Personality. Recognize higher levels of Being in yourself as well, and direct your attention there. This will aid in discernment.

7

VANITY

QUESTION:

When another is attentively listened to or 'seen' in situations where I am not, I immediately feel negativity towards them. I resent that they are heard and I am not. I feel either my 'ideas' are just as important as theirs are so 'it is not fair'.

RESPONSE:

Resentment toward another because they have what you do not, i.e. attention, appreciation, is nothing more than envy and offended Vanity. Your ideas may indeed but to whom does it matter? To you? Or can your concern be for the betterment of the whole group, the other individual, or the situation? So what if someone is getting more attention than you are? Maybe they need it. Maybe they need it even more than you need it, and maybe you could give up your own desire for it as an exercise in External Considering. Don't expect "fairness", it isn't reasonable.

QUESTION:

When another person is walking ahead of me, blocking my path, not seeing me, I become irritated. Likewise, when I am speaking and am not heard or when in a group with several others in conversation and I am being ignored, I become irritated or feel isolated, ostracized, self- pity.

RESPONSE:

When someone is blocking your path, your irritation is impatience.
If you feel you are being ignored, ostracized, or isolated, Vanity is
at work. All of these negative emotions exist in you because you
have requirements of the world, of other people, of your life,
and your requirements keep you stuck in all of the aspects of Inner
Considering. Vanity fills you with talk and Inner Considering (Do
they like me? Does she find me attractive? Do I seem boring? Why
didn't that person answer my question? Am I laughing too loud?
Does anyone see the real me? Am I appreciated for my talent, wit,
gifts, looks, etc.? Have I received enough respect, recognition,
reward? Am I getting what I want? Am I satisfied? Am I
gratified?)

If your own view of yourself is dependent upon other peoples'
responses to you, then your personality is governed by Vanity.

* * *

QUESTION:

Nicoll in one of his commentaries speaks of an important
realization one can make that one does not know oneself at all
including what a "thought" or "emotion" is, or where such
"thoughts" or "emotions" come from. Keeping this in mind then as
my question will relate to this. We were given the task sometime
ago to observe inner- talking. I have continued to do so when I
remember to. Nicoll suggests that inner-talking is usually related to
'grievances', singing one's song, inner considering. For a while I
did not see the deeper levels of motivation in my observations of
inner-talking. The last few days I have finally seen them though.
They are NOT as Nicoll suggests but more frequently are the
following- My inner-talk is future imagination. I imagine
conversations with others where I am "recognized", told how
wonderful I am, told I am brilliant etc. , and of course because it is
"imagination" I begin to believe. and I am tempted or there is a
seduction to continue these pretend conversations to feed Vanity.
Well, now, with apologies for the length, my question is. Although

seeing this motivation effectively stops the inner conversations and sometimes I can even stop without criticizing myself. I wish to know and am at an absolute loss to comprehend, "Where do these thoughts come from?" It is not like I am feeling dejected or something, so out of vanity I must create an inner conversation to feed vanity. What is the source of such thoughts?

RESPONSE:

To begin with, to want recognition for being "wonderful" and "brilliant" is nothing more than Vanity and Inner Considering. It is caring about what others think of you and how they see you and whether they value you enough and getting what you presume you deserve. Vanity can never be fed enough to be satisfied. It is in constant need of reinforcement for the Pictures it must uphold. That is the motivation behind that particular kind of inner talking. As for the source of your thoughts, the possibilities are endless. Some begin in infancy, branded into your Personality through suffering or simple imitation or any number of other experiences. Some thoughts come from external stimuli that go unrecognized yet remain in the unconscious and arise through association. Some thoughts are only associative. Some are forcefully impressed upon you. Some come from unconscious connections between I's, etc. It can be helpful to understand the source of your thoughts. But it is not always possible and the more important issue is what thoughts you choose to give your attention to. Are you able to practice "Thought Selection" in relation to this issue? If not, can you practice Inner Silence in reference to particular thoughts?

Nicoll: ""A terrific fight is necessary before this power of Imagination can be loosened, and a great deal of thought and trial and experiment and failure and quietness and patience."

* * *

Vanity is obsessed with keeping score. It has very little humility and needs constant verification that it is superior in some way or another. So you have identified a Chief Feature, now Observe it and how it functions and what it is related to.

* * *

Almost all of the difficulties you are dealing with belong to Inner Considering and most especially to Vanity. You have observed this for yourself, the issue of Vanity. Needing to be "seen", needing to be "appreciated", "valued", "verified" by others' approval, and the invisibility that pains you as well as your need to be understood are all aspects of Vanity. Vanity derives its self-worth from external life. It needs to be fed by constant attention, appropriate valuation, and confirmation that one is important. I encourage you to read everything you can in the Commentaries about Vanity and Inner Considering. These two tyrants only hold you in their grip for as long as you let them.

Inner Considering and Vanity are the natural condition of the psychology acquired according to brain stem urges. Each of us has the need to be accepted by the "group" as a form of self-preservation. This gets translated into needing external validation in order to feel real and safe. However, what is real in you exists already although undiscovered. It does not require any external circumstance to be secure, authentic, and able to function in solitude without feeling lonely. Feeling lonely in your current circumstances indicates to me that you have cut yourself off from that which could free you. Examine the intensity of your need for validation and socializing. Socializing is generally the wrong use of sex energy or simple distraction.

***

This Work is all about developing the Emotional Center. However it is not a matter of reconnecting to Essence. The issue is riding the Emotional Center of the wrong work of Inner Considering in all its aspects. To try and work on the Emotional Center from the angle of External Considering is jumping ahead of yourself. First, you must work diligently on cleansing the Emotional Center of its wrong work. Then you can practice External Considering rightly.

Self-deprecation is just the flip side of Vanity. Also it can be an excuse to not make real efforts. There is no real observing in self-deprecation.

What nurtures you? Not your Vanity Feature. Your heart. What do you find to be sweet in life: animals, plants, children, music, nature, close personal relationships? If you feel this Emotional Center starvation, FEED YOURSELF POSITIVE EMOTIONAL IMPRESSIONS. Please do not chastise yourself. It is only further identification with yourself. OBSERVE. Practice Inner Separation. If you are feeling the "terror" of the conditions you are observing, you are stuck fast in Identification and have no way out. If you can observe the condition of your psychology at present and say to it "this is just my mechanics at work", "my Vanity Feature is asserting itself", "my Tramp Feature is avoiding having to work", "my Fear Feature needs reassurance", then you can begin to separate from the Negative Emotions the observations are attached to.

When you observe objectively an aspect of your psychology such as Vanity, when you observe it repeatedly in all its manifestations you will begin to know that these actions are not YOU. They do not express the truth of your Real I. You will see the futility and indignity of seeking your self-worth outside of yourself through the fickle flattery and appreciation of others. You will grow to dislike this immature dependence upon others' opinions of you. The Real I that is taking form through Self-Observation will begin to assert itself in place of Vanity or Trampishness. That which "knows that it knows" in you will not need external verifications.

I suggest that you attempt to make your internal I's passive and quiet as much as possible so that you can see. If I's and glimpses of states are still moving too quickly for accurate observation, try to grab onto one particular observed I and hold it, letting everything else pass while you examine it to the extent that you can.

Remember that Vanity in Latin is "vanitas" and it means "empty". You are not empty. You are at least seeing some things of value, therefore you can apply the Work to the material you have. "Whatever you can do, or dream you can, begin it. Boldness has genius, power, and magic in it." (Goethe)

***

The I's of Vanity and Inner Considering (needing to feel attractive) are only part of the wrong work which you observed in relationship to "pretty women". This is also a distortion of sex energy called Infrasex. In the case of a newlywed, I find this activity a little more surprising, however it is very common as you well know. It will ruin the possibility of a good marriage and corrupt your work efforts.

***

QUESTION:

If you are stuck in vanity, you are incapable of performing at top notch-- even children can see through it. On the other hand, a humble approach will appeal to the King of Hearts even in the unconscious.

RESPONSE:

Even though we are all victims of constant internal talking someone with a Vanity Feature talks more internally and externally. Externally to keep the attention on themselves, internally because they remain fascinated by themselves.

I have observed in myself being carried along in the momentum of negative associations in conversation with friends. My observation put a stop to my mechanical reactions and I became quiet. I noticed that no one missed my biting wit as much as I did. I noticed that perhaps I had even offended someone unintentionally. I have observed myself trying to impress someone of importance, seeking their exalted approval or appreciation, even notice. Seeing this as immature, petty gratification-seeking produced by Inner Considering and Vanity was in such contradiction to the dignity of Real I that all Inner Considering stopped and my center shifted away from needing external validation.

***

QUESTION:

We have been asked to look for groups of "I's". I have observed a set of "I's" that seem to have the same or similar psychological root. I don't like being insulted. I don't like affronts to my dignity. I don't like being "shown up". I don't like being ignored. I don't like being interrupted. I don't like being outsmarted. I don't like being laughed at. I don't like being criticized. I don't like being talked down to. I don't like being snubbed. I don't like being overlooked. These seem to fall together and may have their root in Vanity.

RESPONSE:

That is exactly right. You can trace them right back to their source in Vanity. This is a good thing to know what you have to deal with and gives you a bit of distance for Inner Separation in realizing that these emotions are mechanical manifestations of Feature.
Now look behind the Vanity. Do you see insecurity? Fear? Or what?

***

QUESTION:

With respect to 'Imitation": I am so ridiculous that at times I even imitate a twitch that a well-established Judge has (for medical reasons I think) because Vanity thinks this shows how concentrated and powerful my thoughts are. Sometimes I unnecessarily limp a bit to show others how "tired" and "hard working" I am.

RESPONSE:

Types certainly do have mechanical responses of attraction or repulsion. That doesn't mean that the phenomenon you experience in relation to Martial body types is because of being an opposite type. It could be as easily a Fear Feature responding to a Power Feature or a Vanity Feature responding to a Dominance Feature, or some other particulars.

This phenomenon is simple Inner Considering, punctuated by Vanity. It speaks to me of deep insecurity and Fear. Most likely, not a single person noticed or cared where you were going. You were in Negative Imagination generated by Inner Considering. You were worried what other people would think of you when it's a near certainty that other people aren't thinking of you at all. They are thinking of themselves as well - wondering, worrying, whether or not you are noticing their Inner Considering. The Work will gradually diminish your need for external validation, approval and will have no response to others' reactions.

It is quite special, an accomplishment to have had all of those I's, recognize them for what they were, and be able to separate from them. This is the type of practice I was referring to earlier and it is an excellent example and effort. You say that you rarely observe. That is where you have to focus your attention. You can see the results in this event. By not going with Negative I's, Inner Considering, Vanity and Justification, you achieve the results both internal and external that the Work aims at.

***

I don't believe your accumulated Work I's and efforts and your Understanding can revert to being weak. This "mocking of the world" is a common game that two Vanity Features play with each other. But as you know the Work is not of the world. Trust that what you have already verified cannot be lost to you.

***

These two characteristics are both very common childhood experiences, being afraid and wanting attention. You may have heard the idea that each of us has a Chief Feature and two subordinate Features that form a kind of triad that can be deceptive. The point here is that you have to Work against Fear and against Vanity, regardless of their position of superiority at the time. Although Fear is crippling, Vanity may be harder to overcome and I suggest you Work on that issue first (Vanity).

If you can eliminate this characteristic of wanting attention (Vanity), you will effectively decrease the amount of Fear you experience.

The first big example I can think of is the Fear of commitment that I see you have. This is so prevalent that it is hardly considered emotionally dysfunctional. It partly comes from brain stem urges for self-preservation. In Nature, the animal that is vulnerable is the one that doesn't survive. But we are aiming here for a level above that of animal and brain stem urges. Also, you have expressed your Fear of being invisible, of being insignificant or unnoticed among other things. These come from Vanity. You are right that it will take Observing from many angles over a period of time to verify this idea if it is true. Whenever you experience the uncomfortable feeling associated with Fear, try to discern its origin.

* * *

QUESTION:

It seems that Vanity cannot be got rid of abruptly...How can we take steps everyday to continually reduce Vanity?

RESPONSE:

Reflect on its source. A person seeking dignity of Being cannot be at the mercy of the emptiness of Vanity. Feeling superior is an inaccurate view of oneself. Acting superior manifests foolishness. Remember especially that it is through Humility that one receives the force of the Work and can receive enlightenment.

I believe your Chief Feature is Vanity and your satellite Features are probably Fear and Non-Existence. This is a complicated configuration. Vanity can't be afraid or non-existent. I believe you have stated in the past that one of your greatest fears is that of being invisible (non- existent) which is a horror to Vanity. You also have a strong dose of Solar to deal with. This makes everything more complicated because the quality of Solar is so ethereal that it has a hard time seeing gritty reality and has to be intentional to be able to deal with it. It is extremely difficult for a Solar to be intentional or even notice that he is not being so.

***

Being concerned about what people think of you, in this instance, whether you know something, etc, is Inner Considering. The fear of being vulnerable can have more sources than Inner Considering, for instance -- Fear Feature or Vanity.

***

QUESTION:

Where does the pleasure in "extracting every farthing" come from, in reminding people how you were "right" and they were "wrong"?

RESPONSE:

That's nothing more than Vanity. Silly, empty, childish "I'm better than you are".

***

Identifying one's Chief Difficulty in the beginning of the Work means Self-Observation. Working on it (Chief Feature) should be in the form of Self-Observation only in the early stages. You have seen Pride and Vanity within yourself and your description of the "Achiever/Doer" is a Picture of Vanity. Vanity is obsessed with keeping score. It has very little humility and needs constant verification that it is superior in some way or another. So you have identified a Chief Feature, now Observe it and how it functions and what it is related to.

8

MULTIPLICITY

QUESTION:

I begin to sometimes see "sub-personalities", where I have a distinct attitude or outlook that arises and operates for a brief time and then changes subtly into another set of attitudes -- these may be "groups of I's" or "habitual sets of I's". It is as if I could give them their own names. These sub-personalities seem to arise unannounced and leave the same way. Observing them seems to help me see them as not "me", but some sub-personalities seem more artificial and some not so artificial and I would like to operate less from the artificial sub-personalities. If I am not able to control their coming and going, what Work approach should I use in this connection?

RESPONSE:

These sub-personalities are groups of I's. Probably all habitual. Observing them, as you have verified, helps you to separate to a degree. This dilemma is addressed in the Commentary on "The Selection of Thoughts". Nicoll: "Eventually, then, I realized that although we cannot stop our thoughts, we can select our thoughts. I mean we can select which thoughts we go with and dislike thoughts that we know quite well by observation always lead to the worst slums in our psychology....We always have some power of selection in our interior world."

* * *

Be aware that recognizing that you are not one I but many,

Multiplicity, is the first taste of real Self-Remembering. When you see the hordes of mechanical I's taking charge and acting without your authority, you get a better sense of what Real I might be.

If you have not observed this string of successive I's, it is only because you have not observed rightly and long enough. This is a fact of the Work which can be verified through observation.

* * *

You are a Multiplicity. You have within you I's that are good, bad, noble, vainglorious, selfish, perverse, honest, insightful, violent, lying, imagining, etc. These different aspects of yourself have relative value and relative expression of what is most true to your deepest Self. Your task in the Work is to learn to discern between what is good and valuable and what is untrue and harmful. Then the next steps will function to eliminate what is undesirable in the Work sense, and you certainly should keep what is real and valuable. Then put these things into the service of your Work. False Personality, Negative Emotions and mechanical behavior will all be lost in the process to be replaced by True Personality, Positive Emotions, and Conscious action.

***

You cannot do this Work as long as you take yourself as one I. You have to observe multiplicity in order to be able to separate from detrimental I's.

"If you take yourself as one I then that I cannot have power over another I."

***

As you Observe the Multiplicity and discern what belongs to Real I and what is acquired Personality. Over time, what is false will fall away and what is authentic and pure will emerge in the space that is made by the absence of Wrong Work.

***

In the Commentary reading for tonight, the most important point made is that of beginning to sense two men in you. There must be an Observing side that is Observing the active Personality. These two are very different in taste and function. It is when Observing I begins to become defined through practice that you can perceive the difference. This Understanding or rather realization that you are a Multiplicity is a very significant stage in the Work.

You can only come to this realization if you have a functioning Observing I that can Verify it for you.

***

QUESTION:

I have been thinking about humility. Monday when you said "make sure humility is what you want" At that moment I saw the different "I's". Part said yes. The others said no way. I observed pride etc. and found fear beneath it. Survival fear...All kinds of memories returned from childhood. The fear seems to be connected to an idea formed early of being too inept to survive. I don't know if this is an overactive mind or real insight yet.

RESPONSE:

One thing to note is that you have Observed Multiplicity. This is an event that doesn't usually take place this early in personal Work. When you KNOW that you are a Multiplicity, this is a definite stage, an important turning point in the Work. Fear will exaggerate and agitate your self-interest. And Humility will do the opposite. Humility is a difficult concept to Work with in Western civilization and especially for men who are enculturated to consider it weakness.

***

To extend the practices we have been doing, try to observe Multiplicity, that is, the Many I's in you all claiming to be you in their turn. Just observe how one I takes the place of another instigated by an event, external or internal. Eventually, Unity is possible and Intentionality takes the place of Multiplicity. The important point to notice is that you are not one I. When you know this, you will begin to be able to choose which I's honestly speak for you.

***

QUESTION:

In the current instance the struggle I earlier referred to between wanting to speak here ("Yes") and not speaking unless I was certain it came from a right place in me and not from desire to belong ("No"). The I's of wanting to speak and not wanting to speak went back and forth more and more quickly. I experienced something like this in Foundation meetings years ago. I would not speak unless I was sure it came from a place of humility. Every time I reacted internally I 'questioned' where this reaction came from.

RESPONSE:

The most important thing to know about where this phenomenon comes from is that it is coming from multiplicity. There is no discretion or unity and too much Inner Considering happening. This experience should not be that difficult. Don't add Unnecessary Suffering. I don't expect all questions to come from the "right understanding". Ask any questions you want. Don't try to screen them. Just talk.

***

Quoting Nicoll again: "You know it is said that the first form of self-remembering is the realization of one's mechanicalness. Man must struggle with identifying with himself and with these illusions and pictures he is identified. He thinks himself one person who has will and full consciousness". You cannot do this Work as long as you take yourself as one I. You have to observe multiplicity in order to be able to separate from detrimental I's. "If you take yourself as one I then that I cannot have power over another I."

***

Nicoll quote: You will only get into a state of complete confusion if you think that you are one I and think in some way that this I can observe this one I. "If we suppose that there is only one thing that acts in a man, then it will be impossible for one thing to command another to obey."

***

To extend the practices we have been doing, try to observe Multiplicity, that is, the Many I's in you all claiming to be you in their turn. Just observe how one I takes the place of another instigated by an event, external or internal. Eventually, Unity is possible and Intentionality takes the place of Multiplicity. The important point to notice is that you are not one I. When you know this, you will begin to be able to choose which I's honestly speak for you.

***

Try to understand what this condition means to the validity of your psychological condition. And be aware that recognizing that one is not one I but many, Multiplicity, is the first taste of real Self-Remembering. When you see the hordes of mechanical I's taking charge and acting without your authority, you get a better sense of what Real I might be.

***

Verifying that one has Many I's is a definite step-in the Work process. The reason the doctrine of I's is so important is not only so that we can Verify our Multiplicity, but more importantly, so that we can begin to assign value to certain I's and give them authority over other I's. If you assume that you are only one I, that one I cannot assert any influence over any other I.

QUESTION:

The doctrine of I's is the most important part of the psychological teaching of this Work because it is here that the avenue of escape lies. The fact of Multiplicity provides the very tools needed to acquire something new. Within the fragmentation of Many I's, Work I's have the potential of coalescing and replacing Multiplicity which can open the way for Real I.

RESPONSE:

This avenue of escape is inherent in the doctrine of I's because it gives you a chance to CHOOSE. If you take yourself as only one I, you have no choices.

***

Verifying Multiplicity is definitely part of the Work on Buffers. You have to see and know that you are a multiplicity. In doing so, you can begin to perceive the blind spots of Buffers. Don't accept being blind.

***

QUESTION:

It is just that sometimes it is like a house of mirrors.

RESPONSE:

That is exactly what seeing Multiplicity is like. And the False Personality consists only of Multiplicity. Remember that Nicoll says that recognizing one's Multiplicity is a definite stage in the Work. It shows real progress.

***

The Fellowship of Friends wanted you to think External Considering meant your being servile to them. The next time you have bad thoughts about someone, look at them more carefully. They are a Multiplicity and they are in complete Identification, and they are sound Asleep in Second State. Their life and circumstances, that you may know nothing about, may be a living hell for them. Recognize that they also have within them different levels and I's belonging to all of them, including some noble and good I's. Try to raise the level of Negative I's against a person
to a level of Understanding. This perspective will free you.

***

Your Personality will resist the Work. It doesn't want to make the effort, but more importantly, it is protecting its existence. I know this seems strange, but it is rather like something in you desperately trying to hold together the Multiplicity to avoid the loss of ego. Sometimes, you may experience only a slight struggle. Sometimes you have to beat the bear.

QUESTION:

I have been thinking about humility. Monday when you said "make sure humility is what you want" At that moment I saw the different "I's". Part said yes. The others said no way. I observed pride etc. and found fear beneath it. Survival fear. All kinds of memories returned from childhood. The fear seems to be connected to an idea formed early of being too inept to survive. I don't know if this is an overactive mind or real insight yet.

RESPONSE:

One thing to note is that you have Observed Multiplicity. This is an event that doesn't usually take place this early in personal Work. When you KNOW that you are a Multiplicity, this is a definite stage, an important turning point in the Work. Fear will exaggerate and agitate your self-interest. And Humility will do the opposite. Humility is a difficult concept to Work with in Western civilization and especially for men who are enculturated to consider it weakness.

***

You are a Multiplicity. You have within you I's that are good, bad, noble, vain, glorious, selfish, perverse, honest, insightful, violent, lying, imagining, etc. These different aspects of yourself have relative value and relative expression of what is most true to your deepest Self. Your task in the Work is to learn to discern between what is good and valuable and what is untrue and harmful. Then the next steps will function to eliminate what is undesirable in the Work sense, and you certainly should keep what is real and valuable. Then put these things into the service of your Work. False Personality, Negative Emotions and mechanical behavior will all be lost in the process to be replaced by True Personality, Positive Emotions, and Conscious action.

9
PSYCHOLOGICAL VERTIGO

QUESTION:

Working quietly in my yard and observing a type of impatience always with me accompanied by a tension in the body. I tried to dissolve the hurry and tension by observation and that and the hard work helped a good bit. At the same time. I knew I was in an interval of sorts and at times seemed like a stranger to myself. I did not fight it and can see the Work Is re establish. Interesting experience.

RESPONSE:

Did this feel like "psychological vertigo" to you?. Because you felt like a stranger to yourself?

QUESTION:

I knew it was an incredibly powerful attempt of false Personality to take over. Like a false Personality Battle of the Bulge. Yes stranger.

RESPONSE:

This is a common phenomenon when false Personality begins to come apart, leaving gaps where you have no functional or recognizable Personality. I've noticed that almost everyone is experiencing impatience with this process. If you could work for the sake of making good efforts and eliminate elements like impatience and frustration and confusion through Inner Separation you would all get better results. Impatience and frustration are Negative Emotions that will prevent any growth or possibility of Objective Observation.

***

We are hearing from some of you about the "psychological vertigo" accompanying this process which begins with the deconstruction of our false personality. This vertigo is being expressed in a sense of panic, a feeling of emptiness, a feeling of fear or anxiety, or sometime the sense of being a fraud. The best way to deal with it is to try to practice inner separation in relation to those feelings and realize that this is a natural, temporary response in the process of the Work. The way to eliminate that negative experience is by building something real internally which will act consciously in the world. The way to build that in yourself begins with and relies upon self-observation.

When you begin to actually catch glimpses of yourself through Self-Observation, something changes inside. You no longer quite believe in yourself or feel comfortable behaving as usual. You can see all of these automatic and repeated responses you have to life around you and you begin to recognize that something is not genuine in them. Somehow, your Personality no longer reflects what or who you really feel yourself to be. And yet, you are unable to change anything. That practiced Personality goes right ahead acting in the same ways, saying the same expressions over and over, expressing the same attitudes and opinions in the same ways, using habitual gestures, postures, and facial expressions.

Once you begin to become Conscious a little bit of the existence of False Personality, through Self-Observation, you recognize that the truer part of you, the Real I that you have, contradicts the manifestations of False Personality and is poorly represented in the Personality you have at present. You feel like a phony sometimes. You feel like an alien to yourself. You don't know WHAT your self IS anymore. Your False Personality begins to cease functioning at times when you are Observing. You are left with no Personality and barely know how to react to life at all.

Everything you Observe in yourself seems artificial. You observe multiple and contradictory I's and you feel only confused because you are unable to discern which I's are real and which are artificial.

It takes time sorting all of this out. It takes practice that enlightens you with experiential Understanding to begin to discern the difference in quality between the lower I's of False Personality and the higher I's of Real I. And it is along the way that you can begin to make choices about what you give your attention to, eliminating aspects of False Personality as you Observe, Verify, and Separate from acquired wrong work.

You can see that it takes "process" for all of this to happen in you and there is a time when it is uncomfortable or even terrifying to some people. After all, you are sacrificing your sense of self before you know what "self" will take its place, what that self will require of you and whether or not you are willing to give it.

This psychological vertigo that a student experiences when they no longer know who they are is real and dangerous. Many will retreat immediately into Sleep because they cannot bear it. Others can get stuck at a point where they can see themselves to some degree but cannot feel any emotional discernment and therefore cannot respond with Objective valuation of what they see. So they cannot move forward to Inner Separation. Some will go down other paths, self-made and inherently dangerous. Some simply turn their attention to other aspects of the Work and determinedly avoid feeling the loss of ego, therefore they lose the force of this Work and cannot proceed to develop in Consciousness or Being.

The solution to this problem is to proceed in the Work. As you develop Knowledge and Understanding, Real I grows in presence and strength. Self-Observation is the function that will provide all of the information for this development. So you have to have the courage to proceed in the Work through Self-Observation in spite of the vertigo.

Remember:-- This is a stage and it will pass.-- Everyone has Real I and it is accessible through the Work.-- You have to see the reality of yourself before you can begin to change. Change is your objective. It is natural to be shaken when you begin to see False Personality in action. Think of it as being shaken awake. Remember that you can "fall back on" your False Personality and let it function on automatic if circumstances require.-- Notice the taste of the state of "nothingness" that exists in this limbo.

Perhaps the best help you can find for this condition of psychological vertigo is to ask yourself "what is it that is doing this Observing in me?" As you seek internally to define what Observing I is, it becomes discernible and gains strength. It is connected to Real I, the deepest part of you, the highest state in you, and you will be reassured.

There is one other effort to make to help you with this condition: Remember Yourself.

***

You will notice that the "frightening feeling" vanished once you were again firmly entrenched in personality through your exchange with the colleague.

QUESTION:

False personality perhaps in a "death panic"?

RESPONSE:

Exactly. These experiences reveal that there is nothing behind false personality, nothing to stand on. Your house is "built on sand." And nothing authentic has been created to replace it yet (true personality). This is a common experience in the early stages of Work practice. It comes from shining the light of consciousness on personality.

Ouspensky himself had the following experience early in his

practice of the Fourth Way: in a letter to a friend, he stated that he did not know who would be writing the next letter (which I) and this frightened him. Seeing our multiplicity and disconnecting with our former sense of self is very unsettling. But we need to realize that "I am not that" and that this is a temporary transition.

***

This confused state, although powerful, is temporary and a common experience in the beginning of the Work. The uncertainty, the loss of identity, and the terror that these feelings create is the "psychological vertigo" that accompanies the state of recognizing False Personality with an undeveloped observing I.

***

From the beginning, you must understand that the process of the Work is difficult, requires hard efforts, and can be very painful. It can give you frightening feelings of psychological vertigo or a loss of identity. The loss of one's false personality, the exposure of the ego, these are all difficult, painful, and liberating. This is what you must undergo as the result of your Work efforts and you should know ahead of time that it is lifelong, sometimes nearly impossible, but of immeasurable value.

We are available to any authentically seeking person.

***

QUESTION:

My personality, as I look back over time has a pronounced acerbic wit, a sarcasm intended by me, and seen by me, as being funny. In attempting to make personality passive I note a pronounced decrease in the clever rejoinder, etc. It is such a pronounced difference that people see it quite clearly and my kids think I am nicer (because I have quit talking and listen). I also note when with a group of people, they are always interrupting and jockeying for position to talk, impress, etc. It almost is getting a bit strange and I lose my easy bearings in the midst of it. I am a bit confused, part of the vertigo thing.

RESPONSE:

Even if you are confused, don't imagine that you are lost. This condition is a natural side effect of the Work. You have witnessed others' sleeping Personalities butting against each other and have seen it for the impostor that it is. You are beginning to verify that you are not like that and do not want to be like that. To deal with "losing your bearings" strive for Inner Silence, Stillness. Be passive and don't Inner Consider behaving differently. This "vertigo thing" can be difficult to deal with but it is temporary. It only needs more time to develop Real I that can function naturally and independently in any situation. One more thing -- There is a place for humor and wit in Real I, True Personality, Essence. But not sarcasm if it hurts anyone.

***

QUESTION:

I was in an interval and knew it and I am much, much better. I, or something, sealed myself up like a bathyscaph till I got better. "Battened down the hatches" to extend the nautical metaphor. Is this an instance, albeit a weak attempt, at hermetically sealing oneself, there was something "there".

RESPONSE:

I don't believe so, unless you intentionally hermetically sealed yourself for specific reasons. Being hermetically sealed is an intentional activity of the mind. I think perhaps you reached a stage where you were feeling that psychological vertigo and going into an interval at that point partially saved you from a total crisis of identity.

10
SELF-REMEMBERING

True Self- Remembering belongs to a higher state of consciousness. Flashes of it, glimpses and brief experiences are possible and can feed Real I. But more often before a person has developed in the Work, their attempts at Self-Remembering will be distorted by a lack of cognizance of True Self, Real I. I don't discourage the practice of Self-Remembering or attempts at it . I would suggest you store your impressions from these experiences for future reflection. In Self-Remembering, the Self you experience is nothing like the False Personality you have. Authentic Being in the context of Scale and Relativity is the true experience of Self- Remembering. Remember that the personality you have is not the Being that you are.

***

In the experience of self-remembering, you will recognize that despite whatever efforts you have made toward achieving it, this experience is a Gift. In the experience, false personality ceases to exist. One knows oneself in one's essential nature, as an eternal being.

The best efforts one can make in order to seek that experience are more about letting go than straining for something.

Removing the obstacles to self- remembering is a more effective way of getting to that experience than trying to do some step by step process mentally. Self-remembering is not a mental state. It is not something you can intellectualize your way into.

If your efforts at self-remembering involve "sensing" the body and making an effort to force your consciousness to expand, then you haven't a prayer of getting there. You cannot "make" this experience happen. You can only make yourself ready to receive it.

Removing the obstacles is done by practicing the psychological exercises taught in the psycho-transformism ideas of the Work. One must do the Work. Change comes from practicing, not from thinking about it. Also, one is only able to receive it by being cleansed of self-interest. That purification is the result of the Work.

The paradox is that, even though it is a gift, one must also make regular efforts to try and remember oneself.

***

Self-Remembering is not an exercise. It is a state Sometimes one unexpectedly finds the state of Self-Remembering as a result of self-observation and inner separation. Sometimes this happens when you are observing yourself and you see that your outward manifestations are all driven by false personality and you have a moment of not knowing what you are besides that artificial personality. A sense of serenity and self undefined may be experienced in that moment. You may encounter something more authentic than what you are observing.

Real divided attention requires intentional effort for the specific purpose of self-observation. Trying to practice self-remembering while looking at an external object is a meaningless mind game. In order to remember oneself, it is first necessary to have observed oneself and created enough real Self to know what to remember. Therefore, in order to self-remember, you must first observe.

***

An experience of Self-Remembering is an authentic awareness of your True Self in higher consciousness with scale and relativity.

Self-remembering is a level of higher consciousness. In self-remembering, we know our authentic worth, relative value and our connectedness to all things. Although this state is achievable, or rather is given to us in rare experiences, it is not something we can evoke or control with a level of consciousness that is beneath it. Because Observing I is connected to higher consciousness, creating a stronger Observing I brings us closer to that state and makes us more available for moments of self- remembering.

Self-remembering is a rare state of higher consciousness in which one is both undifferentiated from Creation and entirely unique. It happens only in rare moments and seldom when we are actively seeking it. It comes to us with a sense of selfhood, serenity, acceptance, and compassion.

Self-Remembering is not an exercise. It is a state. Sometimes one unexpectedly finds the state of Self-Remembering as a result of self-observation and inner separation. Sometimes this happens when you are observing yourself and you see that your outward manifestations are all driven by false personality and you have a moment of not knowing what you are besides that artificial personality. A sense of serenity and self undefined may be experienced in that moment. You may encounter something more authentic than what you are observing.

Real divided attention requires intentional effort for the specific purpose of self-observation. Trying to practice self-remembering while looking at an external object is a meaningless mind game. In order to remember oneself, it is first necessary to have observed oneself and created enough real Self to know what to remember. Therefore, in order to self-remember, you must first observe.

Self-remembering is a state of higher mind uncontaminated with anything negative. What you have been able to "observe" in your efforts to self- remember is the artifice of false personality. Once false personality has been observed, it ceases to function smoothly or at all. Sometimes we are left without the faculties to interact with the world. This state is part of the evolution in the Work and it can feel like "psychological vertigo" but it is temporary.

You cannot get to self-remembering without going through the path of self-observation except for rare circumstances that you cannot control. You have to create something in yourself through the practice of the Work (namely, self-observation) that is capable of experiencing self-remembering, that can generate the psychological conditions for that experience.

QUESTION:

Please relate the interconnection and difference among divided attention, self-observation, and self-remembering.

RESPONSE:

The beginning of divided attention is realizing that your attention goes in one direction only -- outward -- and that you live only in response to external stimuli. The "I" that can recognize this is the first "I" of divided attention. The point of the effort is that through realization and practice you can now have more than one perspective.

For instance, the practice of seeing a tree and seeing yourself seeing a tree is useful only in so far as it confirms that one CAN have divided attention. The aim is to take part of the attention that is normally directed outward, engaging in life, and turn that attention inward to see your behavior and the psychology that generates it from an objective perspective.

If you can do this, then you are using divided attention in order to practice self-observation. The aim of self-observation is to uncritically observe your psychology and your behavior in relation to Work knowledge.

The Work tells us our behavior is governed by mechanics, that we are all asleep and furthermore that we do not know that we are asleep. The overall purpose of self-observation is awakening. In awakening we see what motivates our behavior, we learn how to become intentional, self-transcendent, and authentic.

The process of self-observation requires intentional, repeated efforts over a long period
of time, and it is often genuinely painful work. We learn that we spend most of our time in some kind of negative state and from an objective point of view we see the unnecessary suffering of it, the wrong work of it, the interference of it and the loss of
energy that it costs us. These ideas are strong motivations for change. We see our own automatic behavior which may shock and humiliate us and we are helpless to do anything about it at first. We recognize that every action is motivated by self-interest.
We see in ourselves lying, justifying, manipulating, attention-seeking, competitiveness, vanity, the falsehood of pictures we have about ourselves, the multiplicity of acquired personality, even the corruption of merit seeking in our good works.

When the light of self-observation begins to reveal our inner states and psychological condition, the Observing I is still too weak to change anything it observes. However, repeated observations steal power from identifying with our mechanics, help us to separate from them and form a stronger Observing I which eventually does have the power to affect change.

This is a process of purification which removes the obstacles that cut us off from the state of self-remembering. Self-remembering is a level of higher consciousness. In self-remembering, we know our authentic worth, relative value and our connectedness
to all things. Although this state is achievable, or rather is given to us in rare experiences, it is not something we can evoke or control with a level of consciousness that is beneath it. Because Observing I is connected to higher consciousness, creating a stronger Observing I brings us closer to that state and makes us more available for moments of self-remembering.

The goal is the formation of a permanent Real I which is the manifestation of the state of self-remembering. Self-observation, founded on divided attention, creates the link between self-remembering and the development of Real I.

***

The mystical experience, objective consciousness, what is called in the Work self-remembering, are all essentially interchangeable terms for the same human experience.

***

We must always return to the work of Self-Observation. It's the hard labor of bricklaying. But it builds something.

QUESTION:

Do you intend to de-emphasize Self-Remembering?

RESPONSE:

Only in the beginning.

True Self-Remembering belongs to a higher state of consciousness. Flashes of it, glimpses and brief experiences are possible and can feed Real I. But more often before a person has developed in the Work, their attempts at Self-Remembering will be distorted by a lack of cognizance of True Self, Real I. I don't discourage the practice of Self-Remembering or attempts at it. I would suggest you store your impressions from these experiences for future reflection.

In Self-Remembering, the Self you experience is nothing like the False Personality you have. Authentic Being in the context of Scale and Relativity is the true experience of Self-Remembering. Remember that the personality you have is not the Being that you are.

***

Quoting Nicoll again: "You know it is said that the first form of self-remembering is the realization of one's mechanicalness. Man must struggle with identifying with himself and with these illusions and pictures he is identified. He thinks himself one person who has will and full consciousness". You cannot do this Work as long as you take yourself as one I. You have to observe multiplicity in order to be able to separate from detrimental I's. "If you take yourself as one I then that I cannot have power over another I."

***

It is my opinion that in the beginning movements towards Self-Observation, Self-Remembering can confuse the issue. Later, once you have established a functioning Observing I, Self-Remembering simultaneously will give you another dimension of insight and a taste of Real I.

***

Discovering that "Real I does not need to be respected" can be a shock for Self-Remembering.

***

Try to understand what this condition means to the validity of your psychological condition. And be aware that recognizing that one is not one I but many, Multiplicity, is the first taste of real Self-Remembering. When you see the hordes of mechanical I's taking charge and acting without your authority, you get a better sense of what Real I might be.

***

Self-Remembering is invaluable. At this point it is also premature. Do not expect any full experience of Self-Remembering until you have observed and worked on yourself sufficiently.

***

I would consider religious devotion and reverence to be the best allies to the Work. This is one of the reasons we use Nicoll's

Commentaries for the basis of this aspect of the Teaching. They are particularly religious in nature and make connections with original sources.

***

Nicoll says that Self-Remembering belongs to Third State, but there is a paradox here. Even though real Self-Remembering is basically out of our grasp, we are instructed to reach for it anyway. This reaching creates the receptivity that can experience Self-Remembering.

***

QUESTION:

Nicoll also wrote at 450 "Self observation without Self-Remembering is simply not a good practice. The two things are quite distinct by inner taste and I would be glad if none of you asks questions now as to what is the difference" (On Deeper Self-Observation).

RESPONSE:

This quote is accurate, but Nicoll was not addressing new students. One cannot begin in the Work trying to practice both at the same time. Self-Observation definitely comes first and Nicoll states this fact over and over again throughout the Commentaries. At the same time, when you have an authentic experience of Self-Observation, if you examine it carefully, you will discern a taste of Self-Remembering.

***

Self-Remembering "is raising oneself -- not contending. Contending is another kind of effort. Self-Remembering is a non-identifying with oneself -- for an instant -- as if one were merely acting and had forgotten. One is no longer in a Picture."

A moment of Self-Remembering is authentic and free of Pictures.

***

I have compared this experience of Self-Remembering to be something like a being momentarily on a higher floor in a building. As you go up in levels, you can see farther. When you can see farther, you can see a bigger, clearer picture. Eventually, you live at the top of that building (Higher Consciousness).

***

I realize there is some confusing information, even in the Commentaries, about the difference between Self-Remembering and Self-Observation. My own experience is that what you have described is seeing from the perspective of Non-Identification and that Self-Remembering is not an experience, simple or otherwise. It is a state that belongs to a higher level of Consciousness.

***

If your question is how do you remember to Observe yourself, the motivation comes from sincere desire to change. If everything is fine, that desire for change is less. My advice would be to put aside trying to practice Self-Remembering for now. Focus on practicing Self-Observation which can function when things are fine or not. Just register with your Observations what you see. This accumulation of insight and information is essential in forming the next step in your path on this Way. There are simple practices that can function as "reminders" if you find this necessary. If so, we can discuss it.

***

QUESTION:

I was deeply moved by your translation of "Dialogue On The Path of Initiation" by Karlfried Graf Durckheim and Father Alphonse Goettmann. I would like to pose a question in respect the following quote from that: ..."To love one's neighbor is to help them to discover the three fundamental impulses of life: its vital source, its meaning and its unity. This is exactly what we seek in meditation, face to face with God." My question is, what is 4th Way's stance on meditation. How does it fit into the Work, if it does?

***

It is true that Ouspensky used the term Self-Remembering to describe several different kinds of psychological activity. I take my Understanding of the term Self-Remembering partly from Nicoll and greatly from experience. My Understanding is that Self-Remembering belongs to a higher state of Consciousness, the state of Self-Awareness. It is a metaphysical experience and can only last for a short time when we first try to practice it.

***

This varies. But it isn't dependent on the quality of Real I. The experience is available in full to all. It is simply rarely achieved because of all that stands in the way. It can be a very full, profoundly meaningful, even life-changing occurrence, or it can be a pale reflection of one of these.

***

Accompanying an authentic experience of Self-Remembering is a sense of profound peace and the serenity of acceptance.

Can you see how Reconciling Force needs to be Understanding? This lifts you above the opposites through resolution born of Understanding.

***

Nicoll: "I have a right not to be negative" is actually a form of Self-Remembering, of feeling a trace of Real I, that lifts you above the level of your Negative I's which are all the time telling you without a pause that you have every right to be negative."

***

In the Work, the first shock is called the "first Conscious Shock" because it is intentional and it is Self-Remembering. These ideas have Objective Truth at their source. Therefore you will find them reflected in all Objective Truth, wherever it may be.

***

Another quote..."Now the Work says that we must lift ourselves out of this dark state by acts of Self-Remembering and this, as was said above, requires force. It requires some power of concentration of attention and you will never have this power if you let your force run into this inner chaos, this continual procession of mechanical associations, this stream of images, this formless vagueness that is really our inner state."

You will recognize what happens when you don't let your force run into inner chaos. You experienced it at the gym. Were you able to read this Commentary?

QUESTION:

Yes I did and yes I get your point.

RESPONSE:

One more LITTLE quote..."...He must remember, for example, that by the act of stopping all these mechanical streams in himself he may lift himself up to other influences far higher than he is."

***

QUESTION:

Last night something quite strange occurred, it was very late and I felt energized and connected to something beyond me, to the Work. I went outside, raised myself quite above my thoughts, gazed up at the sky and felt a real connection to both the Work and the energy of what occurs here.

RESPONSE:

This doesn't sound like Imagination to me. Can you say more about the quality of that state?

QUESTION:

I had the energy to stop thoughts and raise myself up. I felt the presence of you and whatever connects those of us who sincerely engage in this strange, unique pursuit. I felt a gap between myself and Higher Forces that just might be surmounted one day. I contemplated humanity as a whole both in the city I live in and then moving out to encompass the Earth and time as a whole both in my life and then moving out to encompass generations past and generations to come. I thought of those who are not yet born who will think the same thoughts I now do and those who have long been forgotten and are dust, who have thought the same thoughts I am now thinking.

RESPONSE:

This sounds very much like an experience of Self-Remembering. Did it seem that way to you? The qualities of Scale and Relativity, connectedness, and your unique Being and its relation to Higher Forces, are all part of that experience.

QUESTION:

It is like a doorway just out of reach.

RESPONSE:

How did it leave you feeling? Can you describe what emotions were present in the experience?

QUESTION:

It left me feeling Energized. Doubting my sanity. I felt in awe of the vastness all around me.

RESPONSE:

This is the apex of sanity. And I would describe it as an experience of a higher state of Consciousness.

***

QUESTION:

Yesterday, I had a wonderful experience. I was at the gym and ,as I was entering, I decided to try an experiment. I told myself that working out didn't really require the use of my intellectual or emotional centers, that I should just leave it to the movement and instinctive centers. As I began my cardiovascular workout, I noticed that it seemed much easier requiring much less effort. It actually felt very pleasant. The next thing I noticed is that I was seeing people in a whole new light. I wasn't in my usual judgmental mind, you know...he's too fat, bet he's been working out for years, she's got a nice figure, etc.. I was seeing people and appreciating them. I can't really explain it. It's just that I began to feel delight in just seeing people. The next thing I noticed was that I began to feel an overwhelming joy come over me and began to cry. A bit embarrassing (internal considering- what will they think?) I felt loved and started to feel compassion for others. Again it's hard to explain. Then a song came on the radio, "A Whole New World" from the movie Aladdin. I heard the words for the first time. If you know the song it speaks of a beautiful new world. It was as if I was being told that awakening is possible and this is a taste of what it will be like. This lasted about 15 minutes. Does this sound like it might have been and experience of self remembering? Did I perhaps free up my emotional center a little because I left the workout to my moving and instinctual centers. Any guidance you could provide would be appreciated.

RESPONSE:

In your gym experience, suspending the Emotional and Intellectual Centers allowed you to see in a whole new light because they were available to see. They weren't occupied with Negative I's (thoughts and feelings) generated by the Instinctive Center. This was an authentic experience of Higher Consciousness. And yes, you were given a taste of it. REMEMBER THAT TASTE. Prepare to experience resistance.

11
EXTERNAL CONSIDERING

QUESTION:

As I walked through a grocery store, I decided to try to act from External Considering. As soon as I turned into an aisle and saw someone coming my way down the middle of the aisle, internally I switched to Inner Considering, by requiring, internally, that they move aside or take me into account somehow. The striking thing about this observation is not noticing Inner Considering, but having observed the immediate switch from External to Internal Considering. It seems to me that the foundation for External Considering should not be based on "other people". It should be based in the negation of self-will and self-love.

RESPONSE:

One of the things you verified is that the power of your Features and Personality is stronger than your ability to practice External Considering. This is because Self- Observation, Inner Separation, Non-Identification have to be functioning long enough for Personality to be made passive and intentionality therefore able to be present. The foundation for External Considering is based first on the elimination of wrong work in the Emotional Center, second on other people's needs. It's a good exercise to practice but what you'll find is that Internal Considering and your own Features and Personality are dominant until you've eliminated and disempowered them to some extent.

***

What the Work desires to accomplish in you is a transformation from Mechanicality to an authentic Self of Intentionality which consists of External Considering. External Considering is the un-self-interested state of being in which everyone else's welfare becomes more important to you than your own. That is self-transcendent Work. This involves the death of False Personality (ego). It is a process that requires efforts, sometimes painful, sometimes frightening, but always enlightening and if you do the Work correctly they lead you to your True Self.

***

Whatever actions constitute External Considering, none require being appreciated or even recognized. Those needs belong to Inner Considering. External Considering has nothing to do with getting anything, even acknowledgment, understanding, appreciation, merit or reward for oneself. That is why real External Considering is the opposite of weakness. There is nothing weak in being able to act consciously, unselfishly in the world. Indeed it takes great strength to not be constantly obsessed with yourself. It takes courage and the acceptance of Necessary Suffering, and freeing oneself from Unnecessary Suffering to fight your way through the psychological obstacles of Inner Considering. If you are successful, you have raised your level of Being.

If you are practicing real External Considering, no one can take advantage of you, nor mock you to any effect. Vanity, Fear, Power features do not exist in External Considering and therefore cannot be assailed. You will have gained a measure of independence from the external world and from the tyranny of the wrong work of your psychology.

The motive behind doing a favor for a friend in External Considering is the friend's need. If that friend doesn't appreciate your favor or outwardly rejects it, it is no reflection on your authentic motive and will not be an insult. To use your own example, cooking your wife her favorite dinner may seem like an exercise in External Considering. But if her need is not for dinner but for your attention instead of the hours you spent shopping and cooking, this is not real External Considering. You gave her what you wanted to give her instead of what she needed. Instead of making you angry, it should have motivated you to find out what she needs and to give her that with no expectation of any particular results. External Considering has no consideration for one's own needs. As a matter of fact, one has no needs in External Considering. The needs of others are the only consideration, which is a manifestation of Higher Consciousness.

Contrary to your idea of examining External Considering from a "selfish point of view from the point of view of first line work", it must be said that the first line of Work is ALL ABOUT divesting oneself of selfishness. It is not "an attempt when in the domain of false personality...to focus exclusively on the thoughts and opinions of others." To begin with, False Personality and External Considering cannot co-exist. And the focus of External Considering is not on the thoughts and opinions of others, but on their needs. If the others show no appreciation or even acknowledgment, you cannot deduce that you have failed, because you have no requirements of them. To deduce that you are not Externally Considering them because you have not given them what they need may be partially correct. External Considering would know what they need before acting and even if its actions are ineffective, there is no failure because the motivation is genuine.

So in the Work we are taught to practice External Considering even when we don't know how, just like we are asked to practice Self-Observation which also has to be learned. But to get from Self-Observation to real External Considering is a long, difficult process of cleansing yourself of the wrong work of the mechanics of Sleep. In the meantime, any exercise of External Considering will enlighten you and you will begin to see how very far away that level of Being is.

***

Real External Considering is advanced Work but it is something a student can DO, at least outwardly. Most other Work practices are about not doing, i.e. not expressing negativity, not being mechanical, or are about inner Work.

External Considering is essential to the development of Being. It is both a by-product of progress in the Work and an essential element in a developed person in the Work.

It isn't a practice of being "nice" to others and affecting a pleasant persona, beatific smile etc., but it and all Work practices are firmly planted in Objective Morality. In the natural progression of the Work, having created an effective Observing I, one begins to see all of the wrong work of Inner Considering. With long term observation, you begin to see that all of your actions in the world are motivated by self-interest, even the outwardly charitable ones are subconsciously, mechanically seeking merit, appreciation, rewards. When you begin to feel the insubstantiality and immaturity that comprise all of the aspects of Internal Considering and if your aim is development of Being, these manifestations begin to fall away. At that point, you can no longer walk into a room of people feeling insecure about yourself without being aware that such behavior is mechanical and infested with features based solely on Inner Considering. It will feel beneath you to be functioning psychologically at the level of Sleep, like everyone else in the room seeking self-gratification. The dissolution of those I's of Inner Considering raises you to another level of consciousness. It takes you out of the stream of social momentum and mechanicalness.

What the Work desires to accomplish in you is a transformation from Mechanicality to an authentic Self of Intentionality which consists of External Considering. External Considering is the unself-interested state of being in which everyone else's welfare becomes more important to you than your own. That is self-transcendent Work. This involves the death of False Personality (ego). It is a process that requires efforts, sometimes painful, sometimes frightening, but always enlightening and if you do the Work correctly they lead you to your True Self.

***

If you are acting intentionally by making your personality passive, then you cannot be exploited or used by others. You are in control. Placing limits on our preferences when called upon to do so can create force for external considering due to the intentionality of the effort.

***

External considering is a huge area of effort in the Work but is basically about unselfish care for others. If you treat the holidays as an opportunity to practice external considering then you will find yourself gladly giving instead of sadly tolerating your disappointed I's.

The world is full of people in need. Some of them you know and some you don't. Who you give to and how you choose to give can be directed by inspiration, circumstances, opportunity, etc. If you decide to be externally considerate with someone you know, then you can give THEM what THEY need, whether that is your presence, your absence, your listening, your help, your lack of requirements from them. Whatever circumstances come to you, if you greet them with external considering, you will find your happiness and satisfaction in being able to give.

Looking at the holiday season from the perspective that this is the time of year when it is acceptable to be unselfish, you will find even more opportunities for self-transcendence and external considering. You can be grateful, even joyous, for the opportunity to do so much giving, whether in your family or in a soup kitchen or even in solitude. This is real Work.

***

What the Work desires to accomplish in you is a transformation from Mechanicality to an authentic Self of Intentionality which consists of External Considering. External Considering is the unself-interested state of being in which everyone else's welfare becomes more important to you than your own. That is self-transcendent Work. This involves the death of False Personality (ego). It is a process that requires efforts, sometimes painful, sometimes frightening, but always enlightening and if you do the Work correctly they lead you to your True Self.

***

Recognizing Inner Considering becomes one of the easiest aspects to observe after you have studied and understood what constitutes Inner Considering (refer to archives or Nicoll}. These states become glaringly obvious and are very easy to see, not rare, with the effort of Self-Observation. If you observe Inner Considering, probably the most you can do and the best thing you can do is to make your personality passive. External Considering is a long way down the road of knowledge in this Work. But making your personality passive (not identifying with your Inner Considering) has to be accomplished before one can get to true External Considering. Luck plays no part in this process. Knowledge comes first, effort and practice comes after knowledge, and the result can be the creation of Real I. What you need to serve as Third Force or "reminding force" is a strong desire for change and a good deal more knowledge of the Fourth Way Work.

***

Real External Considering is advanced Work but it is something a student can DO, at least outwardly. Most other Work practices are about not doing, i.e. not expressing negativity, not being mechanical, or are about inner Work.

External Considering is essential to the development of Being. It is both a by-product of progress in the Work and an essential element in a developed person in the Work.

It isn't a practice of being "nice" to others and affecting a pleasant persona, beatific smile etc., but it and all Work practices are firmly planted in Objective Morality. In the natural progression of the Work, having created an effective Observing I, one begins to see all of the wrong work of Inner Considering. With long term observation, you begin to see that all of your actions in the world are motivated by self-interest, even the outwardly charitable ones are subconsciously, mechanically seeking merit, appreciation, rewards. When you begin to feel the insubstantiality and immaturity that comprise all of the aspects of Internal Considering and if your aim is development of Being, these manifestations begin to fall away. At that point, you can no longer walk into a room of people feeling insecure about yourself without being aware that such behavior is mechanical and infested with features based solely on Inner Considering. It will feel beneath you to be functioning psychologically at the level of Sleep, like everyone else in the room seeking self-gratification. The dissolution of those I's of Inner Considering raises you to another level of consciousness. It takes you out of the stream of social momentum and mechanicalness.

So one begins by observing passively, externally and internally, and one begins to see the contradictions between external behavior and internal states and notices that the internal state is always some variation of self-interest; the need to be noticed, appreciated, treated well, the desire to be understood, to possess abilities that others value, the need to be right, the feeling of embarrassment and insecurity when these needs and desires aren't met; the bragging and preening of Vanity; the insincere salaciousness of flirting; lying overtly and lying covertly by pretending to be interested, pretending to know when you don't, pretending to care when you don't, pretending to listen when in reality your mind is on something else entirely; manipulations and the inauthentic actions of all varieties. Inner Considering is always concerned with how it appears. This is only sometimes Vanity. External appearances, position, appropriate deference, merit, status, valuation are all core emotions in Inner Considering.

It is only by observing, verifying and working against Inner Considering that one can begin to get to the point where one's every thought and action is not motivated by self-interest. This is where real External Considering can begin to happen. It doesn't happen by focusing "EXCLUSIVELY" on the thoughts and opinions of others. It happens because being divested of self-interest leaves room in one's psychology for seeing clearly and being able to act consciously in the moment.

Whatever actions constitute External Considering, none require being appreciated or even recognized. Those needs belong to Inner Considering. External Considering has nothing to do with getting anything, even acknowledgment, understanding, appreciation, merit or reward for oneself. That is why real External Considering is the opposite of weakness. There is nothing weak in being able to act consciously, unselfishly in the world. Indeed it takes great strength to not be constantly obsessed with yourself. It takes courage and the acceptance of Necessary Suffering, and freeing oneself from Unnecessary Suffering to fight your way through the psychological obstacles of Inner Considering. If you are successful, you have raised your level of Being.

If you are practicing real External Considering, no one can take advantage of you, nor mock you to any effect. Vanity, Fear, Power features do not exist in External Considering and therefore cannot be assailed. You will have gained a measure of independence from the external world and from the tyranny of the wrong work of your psychology.

The motive behind doing a favor for a friend in External Considering is the friend's need. If that friend doesn't appreciate your favor or outwardly rejects it, it is no reflection on your authentic motive and will not be an insult. To use your own example, cooking your wife her favorite dinner may seem like an exercise in External Considering. But if her need is not for dinner but for your attention instead of the hours you spent shopping and cooking, this is not real External Considering. You gave her what you wanted to give her instead of what she needed. Instead of making you angry, it should have motivated you to find out what she needs and to give her that with no expectation of any particular results.

External Considering has no consideration for one's own needs. As a matter of fact, one has no needs in External Considering. The needs of others are the only consideration, which is a manifestation of Higher Consciousness.

Contrary to your idea of examining External Considering from a "selfish point of view from the point of view of first line work", it must be said that the first line of Work is ALL ABOUT divesting oneself of selfishness. It is not "an attempt when in the domain of false personality...to focus exclusively on the thoughts and opinions of others." To begin with, False Personality and External Considering cannot co-exist. And the focus of External Considering is not on the thoughts and opinions of others, but on their needs. If the others show no appreciation or even acknowledgement, you cannot deduce that you have failed, because you have no requirements of them. To deduce that you are not Externally Considering them because you have not given them what they need may be partially correct. External Considering would know what they need before acting and even if its actions are ineffective, there is no failure because the motivation is genuine.

So in the Work we are taught to practice External Considering even when we don't know how, just like we are asked to practice Self-Observation which also has to be learned. But to get from Self-Observation to real External Considering is a long, difficult process of cleansing yourself of the wrong work of the mechanics of Sleep. In the meantime, any exercise of External Considering will enlighten you and you will begin to see how very far away that level of Being is.

***

QUESTION:

How can I know what others truly need, and what if anything do external considering and internal considering have to do with energy exchanges between people? If one has no needs in external considering, then what is the purpose of trying to do it?

RESPONSE:

The way you can know what others need is first by understanding what it means to be asleep and mechanical. You can know by being able to observe in others (because you have observed it in yourself) insecurity, nervousness, fear, withdrawal, vanity, and all forms of Inner Considering and wrong work of human psychology.

"...and what if anything do external considering and internal considering have to do with energy exchanges between people?"

Let's take an example: If you are with a group of people and you are all operating fully in False Personality, then each of you has self-interest as motivation for your personal agenda which forms requirements of this event. You each want to be appreciated, behind your empathic interest with the others may even be the intent of being seen as amiable and as a good person or a compassionate friend. You're worried if you still have garlic on your breath from lunch. You're resenting someone's inattentiveness or perceived insult. You want to make your point. You want your point to be heard, understood, and validated by everyone so that you know that you're right and so that they know that you are right. You're flirting with someone who is married and you are insulted when they don't flirt back. You wonder what's wrong with them. Then you wonder what is wrong with you. Then you wonder if you are talking too much, or if you really like these people after all. And on and on. There is no useful exchange of energy in this kind of situation. It is all automatic, mechanical, predictable, and pointless.

However, let's say you are with your group of people and you are not in False Personality, which is made up mostly of Inner Considering, what might be going on with you in these circumstances? Might you not be able to see the condition of sleep, the flow of mechanicalness, the predictable stimulus-response behavior, how negativity is contagious, how it most often runs the show, how one association leads to another, how people use buffers, what pictures they have of themselves, what issues they are dealing with, what level their being is, what their features are, what their suffering is about?

If you are in External Considering, seeing from this point of view will evoke compassion for everyone's wrong work, and forgiveness. You could soothe the insecurity of one, absorb passively the negativity of another, include the excluded ones, and generally respond with conscious intentional words and actions appropriate to the circumstances. I hope you agree that this would be a better place to be in. If you do, then imagine your meeting with these people if they were also all Externally Considering. You can freely give to them your attention and care, and they give you back the attention and care that you need which will be an entirely different kind of need than that which comes from False Personality. That is an appropriate exchange of energies between people, each Externally Considering the other. Now imagine the whole world like that, everyone Externally Considering everyone else all through their lives. No fear, no hate, no taking only giving and receiving -- that would be purpose enough, don't you think, to do your own part in it, to be one more person on that side of Consciousness.

***

To try and work on the Emotional Center from the angle of External Considering is jumping ahead of yourself. First, you must work diligently on cleansing the Emotional Center of its wrong work. Then you can practice External Considering rightly.

***

QUESTION:

I was reading today some Nicoll on Metanoia. Attitudes and associative habits of mind. I can so clearly see how they imprison. Isn't external consideration a way to see differently?

RESPONSE:

Yes, External Considering is another perspective. We can put ourselves there sometimes. In the Work we aim to grow into being externally considerate in nature. In disposition, in constitution, in character.

The attitudes and habits of mind that you could see are exactly where you are most identified and least your real Self. Yes, it is about thinking from a new place in yourself that must be created. "Being nice" is often the result, but the point is more about objective goodness.

***

QUESTION:

As I walked through a grocery store, I decided to try to act from External Considering. As soon as I turned into an aisle and saw someone coming my way down the middle of the aisle, internally I switched to Inner Considering, by requiring, internally, that they move aside or take me into account somehow. The striking thing about this observation is not noticing Inner Considering, but having observed the immediate switch from External to Internal Considering. It seems to me that the foundation for External Considering should not be based on "other people". It should be based in the negation of self-will and self-love.

RESPONSE:

One of the things you verified is that the power of your Features and Personality is stronger than your ability to practice External Considering. This is because Self-Observation, Inner Separation, Non-Identification have to be functioning long enough for Personality to be made passive and intentionality therefore able to be present.

The foundation for External Considering is based first on the elimination of wrong work in the Emotional Center, second on other people's needs. It's a good exercise to practice but what you'll find is that Internal Considering and your own Features and Personality are dominant until you've eliminated and disempowered them to some extent.

***

Conscious Love is External Considering.

***

QUESTION:

To what extent is External Considering a matter of feeding Self-Love or weaknesses in others?

RESPONSE:

To no extent at all. That would not be in their best interest. The point of view of correct External Considering is doing what is right and giving what is needed. Reinforcing what is false and weak in another is not doing them a favor. For a more conscious person, there are more choices. In what to do.

***

QUESTION:

Let's put this in the context of one's business, internal and external considering. I can see the point on internal considering always, but the external considering eludes me. I am at a point where I can be passive and stuff with kids, friends, but I feel lost in the business context and this is where my vertigo hits.

RESPONSE:

What is it about External Considering eludes you? The point of it or what it is or how to do it?

QUESTION:

How in a shark tank, to put it bluntly.

RESPONSE:

A difficult task, to be sure. Do you mean that you don't know how to be Externally Considerate in your work environment?

QUESTION:

I do not see how to do it in business. Maybe what I am getting at is function of true personality.

RESPONSE:

Let's say you have an opponent in a court case. Instead of thinking of how you can discredit him, you would psychologically put yourself in his place. This would give you a perspective that you would lack otherwise. It would also give you Understanding, alternative resolutions, and the potential ability to see how to achieve your aim without using violence against your opponent. External Considering in this case would allow you to empathize with the Real Suffering that may be present and be successful in finding a fair resolution. This is the most difficult circumstances under which to practice External Considering and it will a lot of time. Most of that time should be devoted to eliminating Internal Considering which leads in the right direction. I believe this is a different issue than the vertigo of no Personality.

***

QUESTION:

One- Where does this involuntary laughter at the absurdity of negativity (in another or oneself) come from- it caused my wife to become only more negative because I am "not taking her seriously"? and. Two- The "turning away from my wife" and "continuing to pretend to be negativity"- it is clearly pride and "saving face", being unwilling to show another that I have seen my foolishness...can you further instruct me on this?

RESPONSE:

The involuntary laughter is a release of the energy detached from Negative Emotions and Identification. Being unwilling to expose your foolishness (something we all have), is another manifestation of the fear of being vulnerable. Having a Non-Identified relationship to yourself gives you great freedom of movement and flexibility so that making mistakes, being wrong or appearing foolish create no negative response in your psychology. In relation to your wife, External Considering would be to be totally honest with her . It is important to her that you take her seriously, just as it would be important to you . Your Aim is to reassure her, be authentic and compassionate.

***

If you haven't already, read page 253 in Volume 1 "Internal Considering and External Considering". A person of low Being has no Magnetic Center and has self-interest as his every motivation and gratification-seeking behind his every activity. What he/she is capable of in a moral sense defines the level of Being of that person. A man of low Being would be the person who passed by the wounded man in the story of the Good Samaritan or perhaps a person with an even lower level of Being would stop and steal from the helpless man. The Good Samaritan is a man of higher Being who does Good from seeing the good of doing it.

***

QUESTION:

It seems to me that the ability to Love all of mankind requires transformation. Is External Considering a near aim or a far aim?

RESPONSE"

External Considering is a far aim and requires considerable foundational Work on Internal Considering. I think that the ability to Love all of humankind requires a degree of compassion that is as deep as your own pain. Do you love a child who misbehaves out of ignorance? Of course. Transformation can create Conscious Love in a permanent state. Conscious Love also exists now, in time, above you. If it were in your power, would you not forgive everyone everything, knowing now what Sleep is?

QUESTION:

I would.

RESPONSE:

That is Conscious Love. Do it one person at a time.

QUESTION:

This includes, I suppose, the ability to forgive oneself as well?

RESPONSE:

Absolutely. And probably first.

***

First of all, the direction toward External Considering is the path directly through Internal Considering. I have paradoxical perspectives about the issue of the "oneness" of everything. There are verifiable levels where all of life on Earth, all of humanity, all of the Universe are "of one thing". There is also the reality of individual uniqueness. While we share more similarities with each other than we recognize, our uniqueness is like the package that incarnates the different contributions each can make.

QUESTION:

So finding commonness is not the way toward External Considering.

RESPONSE:

When I see another person, I think "there is another person like me". Not part of me, under the same laws, sharing the common experience of life on planet Earth.

Finding commonness is not the way toward External Considering although you will find that common experience will help you empathize, which is necessary in External Considering. As a matter of fact, the opposite is more true. When you are outside of the "common" experience of life due to the Work, it is the growing separation from that part of you which is like the other person which gives you even greater compassion because of greater Understanding and realization that Awakening gives you opportunities that are not available otherwise.

QUESTION:

Could one say," I forgive them because they know not what they do. Being asleep, they know not. Is this a branch of External Considering?

QUESTION:

So External Considering is more like the ability to 'step inside someone else's skin' regardless of your own uniqueness or Level of Being.

RESPONSE: This is definitely the right attitude. But it is only the beginning movement of External Considering.

"Standing in someone else's shoes" i.e. seeing from their perspective, is part of External Considering. Your uniqueness has nothing to do with it but your level of Being certainly does. A development of Being is necessary before you can Externally Consider each person according to their need.

This is meant to be an Objective perspective. Done right it does not involve Identifying. If it leads to sympathy, just Verify whether it is the right Work of the Emotional Center.

Only the small I's can become Identified. Objective I, Real I does not Identify and is the I that is present in the act of External Considering.

"In regards to sleeping machines" that is like asking what use is it trying to be good when my purpose is being good.

***

Do not think that you can use Work exercises to benefit yourself apart from awakening. This is what you owe: External Considering for the purpose of contributing goodness to the world.

***

QUESTION:

Am I headed in the right direction. if I try to fulfill a need I see in someone. even if I sense that this is an ego need?

RESPONSE:

This isn't directional, but it can sometimes be appropriate to Externally Consider another by pacifying them as long as it causes no harm.

Nicoll: "In the Work, external considering must go more deeply than in life. It really belongs to the purification of the Emotional Center. One of the great objects of this Work is to awaken the Emotional Center which is drugged with negative emotions and all the small emotions of self, of vanity, of self-conceit, etc. "...We have to be fair "in ourselves" to others and this really is Work on oneself that takes the form of external considering. A cluster of unpleasant thoughts and feelings about another person, that you have allowed to enter consciousness willingly can begin to grow. It is both for the sake of yourself and the other person that something must be done -- that is, that you must Work on yourself to neutralize, as it were, this powerful material in you. "All your intelligence and sincerity and Work Memory will be required probably to neutralize this poison, so that you can once more treat the other person fairly inside yourself. You will have to drop all self-justifying, and above all you will have to remember what you have observed in yourself and what you are like, before you criticize so easily this other person."

***

The best way to "exercise" your Being is in External Considering. External Considering, done rightly, will increase your Being.

***

External Considering is a powerful exercise as you have now Verified. Eventually, in the Work, it can become a permanent state of Being.

***

Last meeting you asked "what is the best way to diffuse old accounts?" First, you need to decide if you really want to. If you do, begin by realizing that part of the basis of account-making is thinking that others should be different. Putting yourself in the place of a parent, for instance, means understanding what it is like to be him and live his life. It is really the only way to get to Forgiveness. If that parent was a victim of abuse or is limited by any factor, you must experience what that was like for him. You must also experience what you are like to him, from his point of view.

***

QUESTION:

In conjunction with the External Considering exercise, I notice that in ordinary inner-considering, there are a lot of negative "I"s surrounding my relationship and when I make the effort to

External-Consider, those negative "I"s are raised to a better place.

RESPONSE:

Does this mean that you were able to Verify not only the result of External Considering, but the existence of different levels within yourself?

QUESTION:

Yes...This does indeed prove the different levels and that the levels can be worked with.

RESPONSE:

You seem to have successfully combined two Exercises. That of External Considering and raising Negative I's to a higher level. That these levels can be worked with is an extremely important point to know organically.

***

I believe the state you are seeking is one of Non-Identification. It has to begin with self-knowledge and proceed through the Work process all the way to External Considering. During this process, you would become Objective in relation to your emotions regarding the divorce. Part of what you would want to aim at would be canceling old accounts which would require real forgiving. This is a tall order for anyone.

While it is infinitely better to have a relationship with someone who shares the same Understanding and interest and values, such as would be the case with another in the Work I find it to be true that the common knowledge and aims of people in the Work allows them to have a greater degree of Understanding in their relationship, this is not a critical element (sharing the Work) in any relationship. Certainly, children cannot be involved in Work. And since the Work eventually produces an authentic Being capable of External Considering, you can have real relationships, deep relationships, love relationships with anyone.

***

QUESTION:

In my efforts to externally consider my mate we hit a point where she was sure about a course of action and I was just as sure about a different way to handle the situation. Does external considering mean to give in when I am sure I have the best way to handle the event?

RESPONSE:

External Considering doesn't mean that you have to "give in". But think of it this way. If you are Externally Considering another, GIVE is all that is present. Whether your solution is superior or not is irrelevant. I don't mean that you should always forgo your judgment in being conciliatory, and each situation would have to be dealt with individually. If for instance "your way" is better for all and the other way leaves open the possibility for harm, then you have to find a way to do what you know the right thing to be.

***

QUESTION:

Is there a connection between caring and external considering?

RESPONSE:

In the Work, there is no way to Externally Consider another person without caring. External Considering is all about caring for another person's well- being.

***

You can stop the thoughts, the internal words that express worry.

But worry is Emotionally- Centered and therefore it is the Emotions that must be changed.

A quote, "To formulate clearly...helps to prevent this state of disorder. External Considering is always conscious and since this requires directed attention, it takes you out of worrying."

12

NEGATIVE EMOTIONS

QUESTION:

I noted an extremely persistent negative state this a.m. and observed it persistently. I also noted that I regarded it as the most appropriate, or "honest" response.

RESPONSE:

This phenomenon is nothing more serious than falling back into habitual emotional states. If you can do nothing more than observe the power of habit and the psychology's way of justifying mechanical activity, you have some material to work with. Are you willing to let external influences dictate your reality, your states, with nothing in you unaffected and detached from the stimulus-response level of being? Sometimes observing negative states gives you a lot more information to work with than turning away from it. Try to perceive what is behind an habitual emotional state. Do you feel more "yourself" when you go with your mechanics? Do you feel justified in feeling morose, in brooding, in letting your negative half have free rein? This is self-justification, a powerful aspect of False Personality. Instead of allowing yourself to feel justified in your negativity, just look at it. What is it? Where does it come from? Where did it start? What does it give you? When you notice a typical negative state claiming your life, try to stop the negativity before the momentum has a firm hold on you. Look at this phenomenon from a distance as if you were above the I's that are creating the state.

In the Work, the proper way of dealing with Negative Emotions is first of all, not giving expression to them. This you know and can manage. It is critical that Negative Emotions are not repressed as opposed to expressed. They require another approach. Repression will not work in the long run. Observing your Negative Emotions comes next, or at the same time. Recognizing what your Negative Emotions are in the context of the Work and where they come from is the next step. Separating from your Negative Emotions is the next (super) effort and this is repeated until you are no longer Identified with your Negative Emotions. Use the "rising fire of negative emotions" as an alarm. You are in Wrong Work. Stop. Consider. And adjust your attitude to alignment with the Work.

* * *

Ways to Work against habitual Negative Emotions: -- Even before you understand what it is you are trying to do or why, you are asked by the Work not to express Negativity. -- Recognize that regardless of any justification or secret liking of them, being in the Work, doing the Work, means getting rid of them. -- Be aware that they are hyper-Identified.-- Be aware that they are subjective, apply Scale and Relativity. -- Be aware that Negative Emotions are behavior patterns and associated sets of I's laid down in you when you had no choice. -- Know that you want to choose. -- Want to choose change. -- See what destruction and pain they create. -- Learn the taste of them. -- Learn to dislike the taste of them. -- Choose a specific, verified habitual Negative state to apply these practices to: practice Inner Stop to behavior and thoughts that support them. -- Practice Inner Silence in relation to them specifically .-- Do not give them your words externally or internally. -- Make your Personality passive. Don't allow it to act mechanically. -- Sacrifice requirements. -- Understand that Negative Emotions lie, they NEVER tell the whole truth of a thing and cannot be Objective. -- They hold a sort of attraction because of their intensity, which is an illusion that wastes energy. -- Desire to be free of that burden. -- Nourish and nurture your Emotional Center in positive ways. -- Remember yourself.

***

QUESTION:

Your comments on the Doom mentality were quite accurate. I have had friends observe this in me and today I got quite sick and negative to the whole cyclical detail of it became so obvious to me. I am anxious to deal with the problem with the increased energy I have lately. I am just sick of it, quite frankly. It is boring.

RESPONSE:

Only you can tell whether or not this Doom mentality is a manifestation of Fear Feature or whether it comes from another source. Parents very often instill this attitude in their children. Either by BEING the doom around the corner or expressing their own fear. So this can also be a part of imitated Personality. The same goes for worry. You will have to discern within yourself whether or not Fear is an underlying motivation in more than just these two expressions. The most direct route to eliminating all of the Wrong Work of Fear is by recognizing the pointless waste of energy in Negative Imagination. Step away from all of those emotions toward Humility, and acceptance. Practice Inner Stop. Do Work in another Center. And Observe.

I had a very long struggle with Fear, especially doom scenarios. When I understood through the Work that it was Negative Imagination at work and I did not have to consent to view those scenarios. Since those scenarios were such frequent visitors, I was able to turn the situation around. Every time one came to mind, I used it as a reminding factor to not pay attention to the I's. Using your Feature as a reminding factor to separate from your Feature is especially powerful. Consider this Feature the enemy (i.e. a key source of Identification which will keep you from freedom and from awakening). Search and destroy this aspect of your Personality by seeking out its source. First, you have to admit it to yourself, then you begin to see it more frequently, then you can no longer tolerate it, then you separate and study. Eventually, you uproot it, even if some mild forms of it remain. For instance, even if the blood rushes to your face in reaction to confrontation, if you are removed from the Fear itself you can keep your inner state from being as affected as your physical state.

***

QUESTION:

It seems that I place myself in situations which feed fear and I seem unable to place myself in situations which are devoid of fear . I always paint myself into a corner.

RESPONSE:

You may have to make more intentional efforts at becoming passive to your Features. Remember that the Fear is IN YOU and that it is a Negative Emotion that you must not feed. Here is where you can make a choice about what you give your attention to. Insist that you avoid fearful impressions. When fearful Emotions arise, Separate from them and Observe where they came from.

***

QUESTION:

This issue of "violence" seems fundamental. Irritation...impatience, Everything that fouls us up emotionally largely can be traced to this, at least in my psychology. Even the fear can turn into it in a moment. Is this staving off of violence not fundamental?

RESPONSE:

Staving off violence is absolutely fundamental from the very beginning of the Work. You will notice that irritation, impatience, and other Negative Emotions that lead to violence are all the results of having requirements that are unmet. One of the important reasons we begin in the Work by not expressing Negative Emotions is that any one of them can lead in a descending octave all the way down to the most violent states and actions. It doesn't seem possible that irritation could lead to murder. But this is so. It can, it does when it goes unchecked.

***

Photograph Negativity as the Wrong Work of the Emotional Center and recognize from your Work knowledge that negative states lie.

***

Don't try to differentiate between Negative I's. Try to separate from them. Differentiating makes no difference. Separating does. If the I is negative, it is Wrong Work and must stop.

All negativity is the enemy of your true Self. It almost invariably comes from self-interest. Negativity and self-interest are fundamental aspects of Acquired Personality, and inhibit the development of Real I.

Negative I's waste energy, and create momentums that can ruin a whole day. If you can't make them be quiet, refuse to listen to them.

You must be mercilessly honest about what you sees within. It is critical not to justify the behavior that is witnessed.

Separation and non-identification with these I's are the only path to liberation from them and their vicious cycles.

You must have noticed by now that Negativity drains your energy. If you have a Time Body glimpse of what the expressions of Negativity have cost you in terms of wasted energy and lost opportunities, you may find yourself another Conscious Shock to assist you in separating from Negativity and Identifying.

***

QUESTION:

I observe that the non-expression of negative emotions is

sometimes followed by a greater feeling of Essence arising. Is it true that the non-expression of negative emotions can prompt Essence to surface?

RESPONSE:

I would describe the experience like this: the energy of Identification that is in negative emotions is released or detached from the Identification. As a result you may experience a feeling of freedom, liberation, and a lightness of being that is the result of this energy being available to give you a moment of experience of a higher state. This higher state is closer to Essence but is not Essence.

***

People seem to enjoy being made to feel sad or afraid and any other number of negative emotions. This is because Negativity has more energy in it than an ordinary state. The vehicle for this phenomenon is Identification. People in the Work are taught to develop a distaste for Negative Emotions and Negative States and Negative Impressions.

***

In every case of negativity, separating from the force of it will release the energy that would have been otherwise consumed by the identification. If you do not practice some degree of inner separation when it comes to your negativity, you waste the vast majority of the force that could be available to you for use in attaining higher states.

***

QUESTION:

Without Self-Observation in these moments, we simply roll out the familiar and predictable course which leave us with no insights and others with the stale effects of our inner filth.

RESPONSE:

This is accurate. A sleeping psychology can begin at a point where one Negative I starts a train of associative Negative I's that has its own momentum and can lead all the way down to the lowest level in a person. Violence.

Example: I hate getting up in the morning. My job drives me crazy. It takes all my energy. I'm so exhausted. I just need some rest. I can't get any rest. I always have something to do! I wish I could get away from all this pressure, but I never get a chance like that. I have to work and then work some more while some people can take off whenever they feel like it. Why can't I get a break? I've always been so overwhelmed with responsibilities. My life is so unfair. It makes me furious that my sister can travel when she wants to and I have to always be the one to be responsible. Well, I've had enough. I can't take it anymore. I have to have a break or I'll die. If I don't get a break, I'll lose my mind.

This descent into Negativity CAN really lead a person to insanity, suicide, or murder.

So the first I of Negativity is always the first moment of possible violence.

***

If you trace most Negative I's all the way to their origin, the origin will tell you something about yourself and will Verify the lack of validity that these I's possess. For instance, if you Observe a repeated negative habit and you recognize that it is imitation because your parent does the same thing. It is immediately robbed of its substance, of your ownership. It can dissolve in the presence of this knowledge.

***

QUESTION:

I highlighted as a significant idea contained in the Commentary. "In the Work, the enjoyment of negative states must be observed sincerely, especially the secret
enjoyment of them. You cannot separate yourself from what you have a secret affection for." This seems connected to the idea of "deeper Self-Observation" and moving it to the level of seeing motivations.

RESPONSE:

This is exactly right. Observing that you secretly enjoy a negative state is one step deeper than Observing that you are in a negative state. This process continues to deepen until you can see motivations.

* * *

QUESTION:

It has been quite unmistakable. I was in a world of identification with several matters and still caught up in it. It was a very new experience and I just sat there and let the
negativity flow through like a current. I am unsure if I could have stemmed it with effort. Was the process correct in just letting it happen and observe?

RESPONSE:

When you were letting the negativity flow through you, were you experiencing Negative Emotions yourself?

QUESTION:

Not entirely. It was a completely new thing to feel negative but not to be negative, if you can see what I mean. I was emotionally on an even keel, but I felt the onslaught.

RESPONSE:

This is a new stage. The difference between your feeling negative and not being negative is Inner Separation, the beginning of Non-Identification, and the growth of Observing I.

QUESTION:

It is a definite new state for me. Very new.

RESPONSE:

Try to remember the taste of Identification so that you can recall it when you experience it again. The letting things go by or through you without snagging your Emotional Center while you are observing, is a new level of clarity.

***

The Fourth Way is in life and requires that we deal with our circumstances, whatever they are, from the angle of doing the Work. If you feel lost, confused, empty, in darkness -- 1) recognize these as negative states that exist in you. 2) remember that negative states lie because they aren't the whole truth of the matter with scale and relativity. 3) don't try to do anything about your negative feelings other than observe them uncritically and don't express them.

If you are not successful, keep trying, keep doing the Work. Earnest efforts will gradually create a stronger Real I in you.

If you can recognize that your negative states are caused by the requirements you have (of the world, of people, of your life) in order to feel satisfied, then you will know that these requirements are based in Acquired Personality and inner considering.

We Work against these by making Personality passive, by inner separation, by non-identification, by recognizing that inner considering is only self-interest, by sacrificing your need to be gratified.

All anyone can do for a very long time is practice self-observation. Observing negativity is one of the most informative ways to gain understanding about yourself and about the nature of Sleep. You can use the feeling of negativity to remind yourself to observe: How are you negative? What is the source of your negativity? Anger, pain, fear? Make a practice of observing your negativity.

***

The Work exists to give you the chance to find meaning. I could tell you to observe how your bad state is directly related to your requirements not being met and the negative emotions of disappointment and frustration. But what I want to say to you is to find love and fill your life with it. Love IS meaning. Now the real secret...giving love is what fills the emptiness, not receiving love. Things you can do: --Get a puppy or a kitten and give your heart to it --Help someone in need because you can --Be kind always --Be patient. Gurdjieff said "Patience is the mother of Will. If you have no mother, how can you be born?" --Do not indulge the wrong work of the emotional center by feeding it impressions that will "inflame" wrong work. --Direct your attention intentionally to something that soothes you and is a positive impression. Distract your mind with directed creative imagination, work, hobbies. Meditation, contemplation, prayer.

***

Suffering does not run the world. Negative energy runs the world. People use unnecessary suffering as justification for these negative emotions that run the world.

***

QUESTION:

I also feel that the time is approaching when I will need to make contact with others in the work, and feel frustrated at my extreme isolation. I'm sure there is no simple solution to this quandary, and don't mean to impose on you unnecessarily, but if you have any suggestions of how my preclusion from the second and third lines of work might be mitigated, I would appreciate your advice.

RESPONSE:

It would be wonderful to be able to find individuals or groups interested in this Work with whom you could share ideas and understanding. You should search for this. In my experience, I have found that nothing of the sort exists. Indeed, virtually every group or individual connected with the Work manifests some type of distortion usually related to interest in gaining personal power or the need to feel superior. Nevertheless, I would suggest that you not be discouraged by this and continue to seek people with whom you can share the Work. Feeling frustrated at being isolated may be understandable, but then you must look at it also as a state of negativity. This negativity can cut you off from the possibilities that may exist in your isolation. Let your higher emotions inform you and act accordingly. Don't let negative emotions confuse you and steal your life. When the time is right for you to do whatever you decide to do next, you will know. Then follow your Aim.

***

QUESTION:

The system proposes that in our work on ourselves we should employ a key technique that promises to provide material for observation while at the same time presents opportunities for change of being: the non-expression of negative emotions. The non-expression of negative emotions is said to be useful in and of itself due to their entirely self-generated and imaginary quality and that negative emotions simply represent the wrong work of a tainted machine. Secondly, negative emotions are said to be the greatest source of leaks of energy for the machine; a rarefied energy that is best preserved for work efforts. Third, it is said that the energy produced by this volatile emergence of negative emotions can be converted and placed in service of the effort of self-remembering. It is this third aspect that interests me here. It seems that many things are necessary to effect this conversion. One must first recall that this is a useful thing to do; then one must intervene prior to the expression or all is lost; one must relinquish identification with the surrounding causes; one must intentionally apply the energy to the act of self-remembering; and lastly, the machine must continue behaving in the world. For me, this conversion of energy is more rare than the opportunities given to do so; and yet I feel that this is an important idea in the system. This should not sound like an over-emphasis on this particular aspect but simply one that occupies my thoughts at this time. Is this an appropriate aspect for observation and work?

RESPONSE:

There are many reasons in the Work for not expressing negative emotions. When you begin to practice this exercise, you will first be surprised at how often you experience negative emotions. Next you will be incredulous at your own powerlessness when trying to resist the pull of need to express them. The next things you will probably see are justification I's popping up all over the place. Before we go further, let's clarify what the Work term "negative emotions" encompasses. It means not only anger, but also irritability, sadness, boredom, dislike, complaining, melancholy, malice, criticizing, impatience, resentment, envy, "woe is me", rage, annoyance, bitterness, grudges, dissatisfaction, violence, etc. All of this, which you will observe in yourself as well as in others, is the wrong work of a sleeping machine who presumes everything should suit its agenda and requirements. "Tainted" would be an inaccurate word to describe this condition. As a matter of fact, this is the normal psychological condition of every sleeping person and it's just the wrong work of the emotional center. If you manage to do the Work exercise of not expressing negative emotions, if you observe them uncritically in order to see them clearly, if you can do this for even a moment or two, you will suddenly find yourself outside of the flow of human stimulus-response momentum. From this more objective point of view, whether in the moment or later on reflection, you can carefully look at what was behind your own negative feelings.

Almost all the motivations come from inner considering, self-interest, and having requirements. You only have to observe how exhausted you are after a heated argument or at the end of a difficult day to verify that negative emotions leach energy from you. This energy that is made available from resisting the expression of negative emotions can indeed be used by higher consciousness. But for you to presume that YOU can convert and direct it is absurd and dangerous.

This ability belongs to a very advanced person in the Work whose level of being and consciousness are inaccessible to your own level. The only thing you can do is make this energy available by not becoming identified with your own negativity. You very well may experience a momentary state of higher consciousness, a more objective vision of reality, or a degree of understanding as a sort of spontaneous result of the released energy that would otherwise have been wasted in negativity. But if you try to use it for your own purposes (regardless how well intentioned) you will lose all the opportunity it presents. You are very confused about this process.

First: to think of it as useful is self-interest motivated, which will get you nowhere. It is what we do because it is what the Work asks of us. The results are not to be projected by you, only experienced. You will learn in many different ways from your experiences.

Second: if you are not able to "intervene" and prevent the expression of negativity, "all is NOT lost". You may learn as much, or even more from that experience, for instance how difficult it is to resist mechanics, even for those in the Work; how strong the pull of sleep is. Or you may be able to see what aspect of your own psychology is at work overriding your efforts. If you can see THAT clearly, then perhaps you can sacrifice its requirements in order to be successful the next time. Essentially, you cannot lose anything except your objectivity because you can learn from your failures as well.

Third: Self-observation is non-identified and the surrounding causes of your negativity are all in you. Fourth: Again, and it deserves reiteration, you must not attempt to direct the energy generated by the process of not expressing negativity. It is not graspable and cannot be converted by your will. What is higher in you will direct its use, probably in an entirely different way than you would, for example toward humility. It is dangerous to be in Imagination about the Work. Don't presume that you know how it functions or where it leads. Just keep doing it. Over a long term your accumulated experiences will teach you what you have to work on and your Work knowledge will teach you how. The ultimate result of the psychological practices in the Work is a state of humility that allows authentic being to exist and right action to proceed from it. If you are looking for self-empowerment, you are on the wrong path.

***

QUESTION:

A great source of negativity for me might be expressed as arising from the feeling that others are not noticing me, that I am not seen, that I do not matter, that I am invisible. This in itself is difficult to see. Once seen, it must be remembered, which again, is difficult. Hence I am writing to you about it upon seeing it moments ago. I also posit that this source of negativity may be based on either a fear of being invisible or a belief that I am 'invisible' (that is, 'insignificant') Some examples of 'negativity' or other manifestations that arise might hopefully explain better what I mean- 1. When another is attentively listened to or 'seen' in situations where I am not, I immediately feel negativity towards them. I resent that they are heard and I am not. I feel either my 'ideas' are just as important as theirs are so 'it is not fair'. 2. When another person is walking ahead of me, blocking my path, not seeing me, I become irritated. Likewise, when I am speaking and am not heard or when in a group with several others in conversation and I am being ignored, I become irritated or feel isolated, ostracized, self-pity. 3. Then there is the issue of compensation- in order to compensate for what may be a fear of being invisible or a belief I refuse to see that I am invisible- I exaggerate. I must excel at everything. In the past, as a much younger man, I dressed lavishly. At a younger age, I weight lifted. As a student in University, I wrote essays that stood out by covering a subject as completely as possible, often three or four times the required length. Today, I have my own office in the most prime location possible. Of course, it is never enough and deep down there is often a sense that I am 'faking it' that I am an 'impostor'. All this is from a deep need to be 'seen', to 'matter'. To be invisible is a painful, humiliating experience.

RESPONSE:

In this Work, we practice Self-Observation in order to get objective views of our reality. These glimpses form pictures that can inform us. Part of working with a group in the Fourth Way is accepting photographs, pictures, that others give to you about yourself from their perspective. Please understand that photographs given to you from a real Teacher are not aimed at hurting you. The Teacher's objective is to enlighten you so that you may be able to see even more clearly. Keeping this in mind, photograph Negativity as the Wrong Work of the Emotional Center and recognize from your Work knowledge that negative states lie. Understand that the desire to be seen, noticed, have importance, be accepted, feel appreciated, are all natural strivings that arise from the brain stem urges that seek the security and connectedness of social relationships. So these emotions are not only a natural function of the human personality, but they are the same in everyone, regardless of whether the person has developed a personality that manifests those urges differently. Now for the photograph: All of the emotions that you describe belong to Inner Considering and most specifically to Vanity. In this Work, we try to evolve beyond brain stem urges governing our actions in the world and forming our psychology. With that in mind -- You state: "1. When another is attentively listened to or 'seen' in situations where I am not, I immediately feel negativity towards them. I resent that they are heard and I am not. I feel either my 'ideas' are just as important as theirs are so 'it is not fair'."

Resentment toward another because they have what you do not, i.e. attention, appreciation, is nothing more than envy. Your ideas may indeed be just as important or valuable as theirs are, but to whom does it matter? To you? Or can your concern be for the betterment of the whole group, the other individual, or the situation? So what if someone is getting more attention than you are? Maybe they need it. Maybe they need it even more than you need it, and maybe you could give up your own desire for it as an exercise in External Considering. Don't expect "fairness", it isn't reasonable. "

2. "When another person is walking ahead of me, blocking my path, not seeing me, I become irritated. Likewise, when I am speaking and am not heard or when in a group with several others in conversation and I am being ignored, I become irritated or feel isolated, ostracized, self-pity."

When someone is blocking your path, your irritation is impatience. If you feel you are being ignored, ostracized, or isolated, Vanity is at work. All of these negative emotions exist in you because you have requirements of the world, of other people, of your life, and your requirements keep you stuck in all of the aspects of Inner Considering. Vanity fills you with Inner Considering (Do they like me? Does she find me attractive? Do I seem boring? Why didn't that person answer my question? Am I laughing too loud? Am I appreciated for my talent, wit, gifts, looks, etc.? Have I received enough respect, recognition, reward? Am I getting what I want? Am I satisfied? Am I gratified?)If your own view of yourself is dependent upon other peoples' responses to you, then your personality is governed by Vanity and Inner Considering.

3. "Then there is the issue of compensation- in order to compensate for what may be a fear of being invisible or a belief I refuse to see that I am invisible- I exaggerate. I must excel at everything. In the past, as a much younger man, I dressed lavishly. At a younger age, I weight lifted. As a student in University, I wrote essays that stood out by covering a subject as completely as possible, often three or four times the required length. Today, I have my own office in the most prime location possible. Of course, it is never enough and deep down there is often a sense that I am 'faking it' that I am an 'impostor' . All this is from a deep need to be 'seen', to 'matter'. To be invisible is a painful, humiliating experience."

Of course it is never enough, partly because gratification-seeking has no end, and partly because this sense you have of "faking it" or "being an impostor" comes from a deeper level than the world can satisfy. This deep need you have to be "seen", to "matter" is only painful or humiliating if you believe it is. In reality, it is unnecessary suffering and you can simply let it go with the recognition that you do not want Vanity governing your life and actions. There is a paradox here. This deep need to "matter" can be strictly vanitas (emptiness) or it can be, even at the same time, the force behind the effort to find meaning. Finding real meaning in your life makes all the small I's of self-interest fade into nothingness. The next time you find yourself feeling these emotions make an exercise to turn your psychology around 180 degrees and concern yourself with everyone else's welfare, anyone else's needs. If you are not tangled up in Inner Considering, you may notice that someone else is in need or that everyone else is full of Inner Considering as well. They are adjusting their clothes, worrying about their breath, smoothing down their hair, flirting and showing off, bragging, telling jokes, being vulgar, or anything else to get attention. The difference is that they cannot see this. You have seen and so you have made the first step in the possibility of self-transformation. Seeing is the first step to change if you are willing to.

***

In the Work Violence is at the bottom of a degenerating spiral of Negative Emotions. It is the most base and coarse energy. This is partly why one of the first exercises in the Work is to not express Negativity. Negative I's associate to other Negative I's which lead down habitual paths of negative thoughts and emotions. If this descent is not stopped by Non-Identifying, it can lead all the way to murder or suicide. The Work also has an expanded definition of Violence that includes insisting, coercing, extorting, causing harm to someone through manipulation, forcing your will or opinions on others, intolerance, slander, and hatred.

***

QUESTION:

At those rare times when I am able to refrain from expressing negative emotions, I can see myself feeling deprived of something I want to do.

RESPONSE:

You are deprived of something you want to do when you don't express negativity. It feels natural to you to express yourself according to your Essence inclinations. That doesn't mean it is appropriate. This particular exercise reveals other Work ideas that will help in the process of Inner Separation from negative emotions. Try not to just repress them. Try bringing in the Third Force of Understanding to transcend them.

***

Guilt is a negative emotion, drop it. Sometimes it's necessary, once again, to retreat and contemplate. Nothing else.

***

Sometimes observing negative states gives you a lot more information to work with than turning away from it. Try to perceive what is behind an habitual emotional state.
Do you feel more "yourself" when you go with your mechanics?
Do you feel justified in feeling morose, in brooding, in letting your negative half have free rein?

QUESTION:

I am afraid this is true.

RESPONSE:

This is self-justification. A powerful aspect of False Personality. Instead of allowing yourself to feel justified in your negativity, just look at it. What is it? Where does it come from? Where did it start? What does it give you?

QUESTION:

It gives me nothing. It ruins the morning.

RESPONSE:

You don't have to let it. When you notice a typical negative state claiming your life, try to stop the negativity before the momentum has a firm hold on you. Look at whether or not this negativity is caused by certain circumstances or is only your habitual way of being. Look at this phenomenon from a distance as if you were above the I's that are creating the state.

***

Worry is a completely useless negative emotion. If you have an issue that needs dealing with, worry will not impact it in any way. It will only obscure your ability to address the issue with conscious intentionality. For every worry I, say to yourself: what can I do to change this? If the answer is nothing, then stop worrying. If the answer is something, then do it.

***

QUESTION:

Why are people, including myself, attracted to movies which can cause emotional states of terror, anxiety or grief whereas, normally in 'real life', such emotions are painful and avoided? What is it that is of value or positive in such experiences?

RESPONSE:

There is nothing positive or of value in negative emotions stimulated intentionally through negative impressions. There is an element in man's psychological nature that can essentially be referred to as awe. It has a quality called "numinous". This quality is rightly connected to states of higher consciousness. People can get a cheap substitute version by creating the feeling of the numinous through experiencing fear inducing negative impressions. It has a faint flavor of something like awe, but it is perverted and creates psychological poison.

***

QUESTION:

I have seen that observing a negative "I" can remove its power momentarily; and only to have the I return seconds later and once again I am in its grip as though nothing happened. Is this successful observation?

RESPONSE:

Yes, this is successful observation. One possibility for this phenomenon is that when you have something specific that you need to understand in relation to the Work, and you try to avoid dealing with it, it will only return in another form to present the same issues or it may also be that you have a roaming band of negative I's that is a kind of detached anger which will jump on any opportunity to express itself.

QUESTION:

Yes, there is a returning to the former negativity, oblivious to the dis-empowerment of moments ago.

RESPONSE:

Don't get discouraged. Part of the reason we observe negativity is to experience the power it has in our psychology. This you have to glean for yourself through applied practice.

***

The process of cleansing the Emotional Center and the development of Real I are permanent solutions to the problem of insecurity. A transformed Emotional Center has no requirements from the world. It finds its being and meaning in giving to the world. Real I knows its authenticity and doesn't need external validation.

***

The easiest aspect of the Emotional Center to observe is Negative Emotions However, since we were just speaking about it, hurry, irritation, worry and anger are very simple to observe in yourself as well as in other people.

The first thing to be done is to practice Self-Observation. You must have an honest, clear picture of yourself and your Negative Emotions and their causes in order to deal with them. The object is to be rid of them. The Work teaches the way to do this. Observing Negative Emotions at once gives you some distance. Observing them repeatedly in the light of the Work will gradually diminish their power and influence and you will have other options and be able to make other choices.

Not expressing negativity holds a wealth of information about yourself It is also one of the Work ideas we are asked to practice from the beginning because Negative Emotions essentially cut you off from the possibility of raised Consciousness and change of Being.

***

QUESTION:

Is there a habitual aspect to negative emotions speaking with regard to breaking the bad habits, as one might give up smoking, for instance?

RESPONSE:

Certainly there are all kinds of habitual Negative Emotions. Sometimes they can be triggered by things as small as a song, a fragrance, an associative I. You think you'll get up early to exercise in the morning, but when morning arrives your first I is "no". You say to yourself "come on, make yourself do this" and still you don't. You think" this always happens. Every time I try to do something I never follow through. I am so lazy, how am I ever going to get what I want?" Habitual sets of I's like these and endless others begin with one Negative Emotion that associates to and attracts other Negative I's. Everyone has their own peculiar sets. Try to recognize yours.

QUESTION:

Are these "I's" empowered by memory patterns? Or rather, do they originate in memory patterns?

RESPONSE:

These I's are laid down in memory patterns. If you recognize a particular attitude that is negative and recurring, you are looking at habitual Negative Emotions. They do not respond well to the kind of approach you might take to breaking an external bad habit. To observe them and refrain from expressing them and to make an attempt at separation from them is the right approach.

***

This is a common phenomenon when False Personality begins to come apart, leaving gaps where you have no functional or recognizable Personality. I've noticed that almost everyone is experiencing impatience with this process. If you could work for the sake of making good efforts and eliminate elements like impatience and frustration and confusion through Inner Separation you would all get better results. Impatience and frustration are Negative Emotions that will prevent any growth or possibility of Objective Observation.

***

Suspicion, which is Negative Imagination, may involve trust issues. "Self-fulfilling" is an idea that is not valid, it is only guilt-tripping yourself and you can let go of it. The way in the Work to deal with Negative Emotions and attitudes is through Objective Observation, gradual Inner Separation, and eventual Non-Identification with the elements in you that are responsible for this Negative condition. Feeling justified because of what you have observed is a paradox because you have observed accurately, but having a negative response to what you have observed is wrong work and it won't lead you where you want to go. Every time you experience this negative attitude ask yourself what requirement you had that was not satisfied. Then ask yourself if it is appropriate for you to have such requirements. If it is appropriate for you to retreat from the world, then consider seriously following that need. Sometimes this is desirable in the Work. It depends on the individual. G. called this Work a "process of individuation" so listen carefully to your deepest cognition of direction.

***

QUESTION:

I often-times find myself unable to resist the expression of Negative Emotions. What is the proper course when observing Negative Emotions after the fact?

RESPONSE:

That depends on the consequences of your expression of Negativity. Perhaps it only requires reflection. Perhaps you may need to apologize to someone or make amends in other ways. The most important factor here is that you do not justify your Negativity or refuse responsibility for the consequences.

***

Anger and revenge on the other hand are only Negative Emotions and you can be free of them with the right Work attitude.

Anger, being such a strong Negative Emotion, is a fast ride down into violence. The speed you refer to is a problem, but it can be overcome by using another emotion to combat it. The higher emotions of acceptance, Understanding, being without requirements (Humility) are some.

***

QUESTION:

This issue of "violence" seems fundamental. Irritation...impatience, Everything that fouls us up emotionally largely can be traced to this, at least in my psychology. Even the fear can turn into it in a moment. Is this staving off of violence not fundamental?

RESPONSE:

Staving off violence is absolutely fundamental from the very beginning of the Work. You will notice that irritation, impatience, and other Negative Emotions that lead to violence are all the results of having requirements that are unmet. One of the important reasons we begin in the Work by not expressing Negative Emotions is that any one of them can lead in a descending octave all the way down to the most violent states and actions. It doesn't seem possible that irritation could lead to murder. But this is so. It can, it does when it goes unchecked. Do you recognize that other Negative Emotions lead also to violence? And can you separate from them? Can you find a place in yourself that has no external requirements in order to be at peace?

QUESTION:

There is definitely a process in that regard that has emerged. You must realize that I have an extremely difficult pattern in this regard. It was that I could go off at the slightest imagining, and this was not lost on others. Nor has the change very meagerly effected been lost.

RESPONSE:

This is good to hear. If you have a Work process in place that is effective, then just continue.

* * *

The exercise that I would like you to all practice this week is as follows: Every time you Observe a habitual Negative Emotion, say to it "this is not I". When you say this, understand that you are asserting the differentiation between Real I and the actions of False Personality. Remember that habitual Negative Emotions are imitations and responses and do not speak for what is most genuine in you.

***

QUESTION:

Say "this is not I" to habitual negative emotions. When I remembered to do this exercise, as I did on two occasions, it had the effect of releasing an ugly psychological weight from me. Joy rushed in to fill the place where the negativity was.

RESPONSE:

This is a wonderful experience and is the intended outcome of this practice. Have you also noticed a distaste for Negative Emotions developing in you?

Yes. But mainly for the more extreme cases. I still seem to relish a general negative attitude. I think my chief difficulty is Negative Emotions.

RESPONSE:

Do you honestly relish them? Don't they cause you harm? Don't they make you feel bad inside? Don't they make you feel less authentic?

QUESTION:

They feel like an old suit that I just keep wearing.

RESPONSE:

Then the only way out is by getting rid of the old suit a piece at a time. One Negative Emotion at a time, Observed, understood, Separated from, will gradually strip away the Wrong Work that hurts you and stands in your way. Every time you experience a Negative emotional state, practice Stop and examine it. Is it habit? How can you disable it? Can you Separate from it? Can you see it as an I that belongs to False Personality and has gratification requirements? Most of all, does it express Real I?

***

QUESTION:

At a former meeting, when speaking of the exercise to say "That is not I" in connection with Negative Emotions, you stated that there is a "vital element in this practice that needs to be emphasized". Can you elaborate tonight?

RESPONSE:

Yes. By saying "this is not I" to Negative Emotions, first you give yourself the opportunity to discern that indeed what is most real in you is not connected to these emotions. You may be able to recognize something familiar like imitation or habit and taste the Understanding that what Real I is in you has no connection to these energies. Inherent in this experience, which amounts to Not-Identifying, is a taste of Real I. It is revealed by the exercise of saying "this is not I".

***

Internal Considering is a big issue for you, Imagination is monumental. And this you may or may not know, you like your Negative Emotions.

QUESTION:

Yes...they are my heroes...I see that...and it hurts.

RESPONSE:

What they hurt most is you, but I'm sure that also pollutes your environment. You must learn to dislike the taste of Negativity.

***

QUESTION:

I received a really big shock when Rebecca said I like my negative emotions!!! WOW....big way to go, anyway...I am observing along these lines and seeing a lot of how true her photograph is. Is there anything else that could be said about this matter?

RESPONSE:

Negative Emotions have more active energy than other feelings. It is easy to Identify with the intensity of the energy attracts and fascinates. There are multiple reasons why people enjoy their Negative Emotions.

***

Remember that Gurdjieff said that it is Negative Emotions that run the world, not sex energy or power, but Negativity. In the Work, you should avoid any Negativity that you can. This is true of the external world, but the meaning of this practice is to remove Negative Emotion from yourself. From your Emotional Center. That means Working on the causes in yourself, not the causes in your life. When you Observe this in yourself, ask what likes it.

Why does it like it? What feeling does it leave you with? This is a real and valuable step for you in the Work.

* * *

This gives me a perfect opportunity to quote from the Commentary tonight. "And one of the greatest forms of dirt is Negative Emotions and habitual indulgence in them. The greatest filth in a man is Negative Emotion. An habitually negative person is a filthy person, in the Work sense. A person who is always thinking unpleasant things about others, saying unpleasant things, disliking everyone, being jealous, always having some grievance or some form of self-pity, always feeling that he or she is not rightly treated and so on -- such a person has a filthy mind in the most real and practical sense, because all these things are forms of Negative Emotions and all Negative Emotions are dirt."

***

QUESTION:

I was impressed by the thought that I have a right not to be negative. Usually, in the past I might say, "I have a right to be negative, if I want to. But, now I realize that I don't really have a right to be negative, but to not be negative. It frees me up from my negativity. Another quote: "To say this phrase in the right way to yourself, to feel the meaning of the words: "I have a right not to be negative," is actually a form of Self-Remembering, of feeling a trace of Real I, that lifts you above the level of your Negative I's which are all the time telling you without a pause that "you have every right to be negative"". I also realized from this lesson that I don't have enough excess energy to waste it in negativity.

RESPONSE:

I don't think anyone should waste any energy. There is so much Work to be done. I'm glad you experienced freedom from some Negativity as a result of this idea.

***

In the Commentary on Negative Emotions, page 162, part 2, Nicoll talks about levels in a person and about how you can choose to live in better states that belong to higher levels or lower states which belong to lower levels in your psychology. Recognizing that within yourself there are different levels of Being and functioning is an open door to a place where you can see what your choices are internally and you can go to a higher level inside yourself.

QUESTION:

I found the inner "slum" idea interesting to contemplate. That there is such a thing.

RESPONSE:

We all have them and we all have to make efforts to stay away from them if we want to live on a higher level.

***

QUESTION:

Today I had an experience that normally would have caused a lot of negative emotions. I had to deal with a person who I normally have difficulty with. In our meeting today I felt a calmness, and a detachment to any anticipated outcome. I was able, to a certain extent to see how I was relating to this person. I was aware of my tone of voice, and my posture. It was a very good feeling. Could this be the beginning of the growth of Real I?

RESPONSE:

When you have eliminated some of the Wrong Work that stands between where you are now and the development of Real I, you can have a taste or a sense of what this "Real I" is.

It sounds like this was close to your experience. Non-Identification clears the path. Observing I had to be present in order for you to see or to notice calmness, detachment, tone of voice, posture, etc. But you probably had some cognition of Real I in your experience.

A higher place makes Real I more accessible.

***

It is certainly true that everyone justifies their own grievances. And it is patently true that Negative Emotions that are justified cannot be affected by the Work. This is the huge impact that Justification can have. It will immediately put a stop to any possibilities for change. That's what makes it so insidious.

***

QUESTION:

Occasionally, Negative I's will rise in me and find expression when I am confronted with situations that typically trigger those I's. However, I have recently been seeing the Negative I's begin to rise and feel like an inner fire that seems to get "caught in my throat," so to speak, and not necessarily find expression. I can observe this and recognize how my usual reaction would have allowed some form of expression but in this case does not. I am then able to continue on afterwards without any feelings of negativity and at those moments I can see the option of External Considering as an alternative Is this an appropriate way of confronting the Work on Negative Emotions?

RESPONSE:

In the Work, the proper way of dealing with Negative Emotions is first of all, not giving expression to them. This you know and can manage. It is critical that Negative Emotions are not repressed as opposed to expressed. They require another approach. Repression will not work in the long run. Observing your Negative Emotions comes next, or at the same time. Recognizing what your Negative Emotions are in the context of the Work and where they come from is the next step. Separating from your Negative Emotions is the next effort and this is repeated until you are no longer Identified with your Negative Emotions. Use the "rising fire of negative emotions" as an alarm. You are in Wrong Work. Stop. Consider. And adjust your attitude to alignment with the Work.

***

Being passive allows for all kinds of possibilities other than automatic Negative Emotions. While it is valuable and true to understand that becoming Negative is causing yourself harm, your motivation should eventually include the fact that you don't wish to cause anyone else harm either.

***

QUESTION:

As I have tried to observe myself, I seem to find fear as the root cause. It seems to generate identification, formatory thinking, false personality, and on and on. I don't know if this is true or if it's my own current dark state of mind. I would appreciate your comments.

RESPONSE:

You have seen clearly into the source of many aspects of the Wrong Work in a person's psychology. You may have seen and experienced your own Chief Feature, Fear. But Fear, whether it is your Chief Feature or not, is at the source of Identification, etc. We fear rejection, being alone, being in need, being vulnerable. We are afraid of failure, commitment, appearing to not fit in, looking foolish, and deep inside more than anything we fear meaninglessness.

QUESTION:

Thank you...Meaninglessness (nothingness). Yes, this fear seems to be the basis of my personality. Without my image of myself there is nothing.

RESPONSE:

All of these fears are Negative Emotions meaning Wrong Work of the Emotional Center and they result in Wrong Work in Personality. You are mistaken, however. Without the image of yourself or behind it, is your Real I[A student] posted this related quote from Thomas Merton.

"Even when I try to please God, I tend to please my own ambition, His enemy. There can be imperfection even in the ardent love of great perfection, even in the desire of virtue, of sanctity. Even the desire of contemplation can be impure, when we forget that true contemplation means the complete destruction of all selfishness -- the most pure poverty and cleanliness of heart."

The result of doing the Work correctly is Humility. Make sure that this is what you want. Behind your Fear of meaninglessness you might find your only opportunity to have real meaning. Don't let Fear steal it.

***

QUESTION:

Late last night I was exhausted after a very long day and arrived home to find my basement is being demolished/repaired, very expensively (!). My wife was yelling at me off and on for some of the evening. Finally, as I was more tired and had an alcoholic beverage, I felt the anger begin to bubble up inside me. I remembered to make myself quite passive, to in effect become empty and non-reactive. I stood up and left the room to remove myself from this situation, in itself something quite new for me, went outside to calm myself and have a cigarette and experienced a state where I WELCOMED and was glad for the following material for self-observation. While alone outside-I began to actually hear a song, to see it and the underlying self-pity-

"I am not appreciated by my wife. I work so hard during the day and here is the thanks I get. It is not fair". But for the first time ever I could stop the song and as I said welcomed it as material, it is a very old song that I normally sing quite loudly to anyone who would like to hear it. Then I saw another old "I"- I would remove myself from my wife, become withdrawn, NOT go back inside for a while as "punishment". Again I was able to put a stop to this Inner Account.

RESPONSE:

What an incredible transformation of circumstances! So many difficult elements and in the midst of them you were able to apply the Work and stop the momentum and direction of Negative Emotions. This is what this Work is all about. It is much more vast in scope but the results are personal evolution, transformation, and Freedom.

***

QUESTION:

I received a collector's threat on a bill that I had already responded to appropriately several times (insurance issues, etc). The frustration was difficult to control, especially with the elements of incompetence and threat. I was eager for the next morning when I would call these people and "straighten things out". Once on the phone, the matter was easily resolved, and yet I had lost a good deal of energy in Negative Imagination about what I would have to do.

RESPONSE:

A related quote. Nicoll: "We think of the Imagination as a light airy nothingness. But the imagination is very powerful -- very real -- like concrete. Pictures are formed out of imagination, controlled by vanity. They are fixed forms of imagination, woven by vanity. Vanity is a terrific force in us and imagination is the powerful builder and bricklayer of vanity. It builds pictures of ourselves."

***

QUESTION:

These aspects of my condition seem more repugnant and unacceptable than before. And less justifiable and less hidden.

RESPONSE:

That is because your relationship to them has changed drastically. That they are less justifiable and less hidden is a very good movement in development. I know that it is hard not to find the Wrong Work we see in ourselves to be repugnant, but as you know, this approach to dealing with such Wrong Work is not effective. Seeing what is repugnant and unacceptable needs to happen in a space that doesn't respond with Negative Emotions. Otherwise, the Negative Emotions will obstruct your view.

Changing that repugnance into Third Force is the genius of the Work. It is indeed the rise of Buried Conscience which you feel.

***

I would like to quote from a Commentary that we read months ago. Re- reading is always an exercise in discovering the progression of your Understanding. The Commentary is on page 1039, Volume 3, "On Violence and Understanding" "Violence is the antithesis to Understanding. All violence has its roots in not understanding another. It is said in the Work that understanding is the most powerful force we can create. So we have to create understanding. All violence has its root in negative emotion. I said above that all violence has its root in not understanding. There is no contradiction in this. It means simply that negative emotions do not lead to understanding but to violence. The Work says a man is his understanding. He is not his size, his money, position, birth, strength or his prestige or distinctions or religion. A man is his understanding. Violence destroys everything in us. To react with violence is the easiest of all things. To understand is the most difficult. Now it might be said that when you get violent you come to the limit or end of your Being. Capacity for endurance is a sign of Being. Small being which only loves itself, soon reaches its limit and becomes violent. In violence, one is totally asleep and has no understanding."

Can you understand better now why it is so important to not express Negative Emotions? They effectively put a complete stop to any potential Understanding. That means no development. And they have the open-ended possibility of descending into the most base violence.

Violence includes thinking Negative Emotions, murdering someone in your psychology, slandering them with your inner speech. It includes all forms of force, coercion, insistence, dominance, and manipulation. One more quote from this Commentary. "I will say, by way of commentary, that to understand one must learn, and learning is to perceive in oneself the truth of a thing that one is taught -- that the thing is so. This leads to understanding. The Work teaches that knowing and understanding are quite different. I may know many things, but may never have perceived in myself the truth of any of them. In that case, I do not understand what I know though I may retain it in my memory."

***

QUESTION:

First, for some types is violence less of an issue? I am thinking of passive types, non-existent featured types who generally "go with the flow"?.

RESPONSE:

Yes, definitely. Violence is more of an issue for particular types,. Active and Negative for instance.

QUESTION:

Second, you speak of manipulation being a particular form of violence. Some (such as myself) depend on being able to manipulate for their livelihood. I am successful as a trial lawyer to the extent that I can manipulate others at times. But this does not feel like "violence" to me.

RESPONSE:

Although everyone, even the nicest of people, have violence in them. The path to it is through their Negative Emotions. Manipulation in the intentional use of it without underlying selfish ends is different than the emotional manipulation that people abuse each other with.

***

Later, when the state has passed, reflect on what the Negative Emotions were that you felt. Name them. What were they saying to you?. Are these I's familiar to you? (Habitual) Are they truthful?. Try to perceive the source of your Negative Emotions. It is inside you, not outside you. Don't Justify yourself. Observe what is behind your Negative responses. Try to get a sense of the "taste" of it. Is it pain, fear, frustration? About what?

***

QUESTION:

Once the habitual negative emotion is identified, then what? For example, frustration because others are using up resources that I work for without my being able to give an opinion on without getting in trouble.

RESPONSE:

Consider that behind this frustration is not just the sense of injustice and powerlessness over the situation, but Fear which creates those unconscious attitudes. Perhaps your sense of power over what your produce feels compromised. The fear of being in need and the fear of having to do without what you need is probably involved. All of these emotions that you are labeling frustration are self-interested emotions. That is why they produce the Wrong Work of being frustrated. The Objective point of view in this specific case is that you should feel grateful that you CAN give, work, and support your family, and joyful that you have one to give to.

***

QUESTION:

It seems that unnecessary suffering and negative emotion overlap a great deal, if not totally coextensively. All of it boils into a bad state, which is most unpleasant, useless and wasteful. It has helped me to realize I am more like a baboon than Mozart when I indulge all of it.

RESPONSE:

Unnecessary Suffering is always Negative Emotions and Negative Emotions are usually Unnecessary Suffering and all of it belongs to False Personality. Every kind of suffering that comes from unsatisfied Personality is what has to be sacrificed in order to make room for purified emotions.

***

Ways to Work against habitual Negative Emotions: First, recognize that regardless of any justification or secret liking of them, being in the Work, doing the Work, means getting rid of them. Even before you understand what it is you are trying to do or why, you are asked by the Work not to express Negativity. Be aware that they are hyper-Identified. Be aware that they are subjective, apply Scale and Relativity. Be aware that they are behavior patterns and associated sets of I's laid down in you when you had no choice. Know that you want to choose. Want to choose change. See what destruction and pain they create. Learn the taste of them. Learn to dislike the taste of them. Choose a specific, verified habitual Negative state to apply these practices to: practice Inner Stop to behavior and thoughts that support them. Practice Inner Silence in relation to them specifically. Do not give them your words externally or internally. Make False Personality passive. Don't allow it to act mechanically. Sacrifice requirements. Understand that Negative Emotions lie, they NEVER tell the whole truth of a thing and cannot be objective. They hold a sort of attraction because of their intensity, which is an illusion that wastes energy. Desire to be free of that burden. Nourish and nurture your Emotional Center in positive ways.-- Remember yourself.

***

Exercise on Negative I's : Find a particular group of habitual Negative I's (they exist in the lower level of your psychological states). Try to raise this one group of I's which constitute a Negative attitude through Self-Observation and Work Knowledge, to the level where you can see them Objectively. Now if you can see these Negative I's Objectively, you can discern by Knowledge and taste what is true and real from what is false. You will see that this set of I's do not represent the whole truth of the matter. They lie by omission and misrepresentation. They will say things to you that, in a higher state, you would recognize are not true.

Everything they say to you, they say to support the feelings of Negative Emotions within you. What is BEHIND those feelings? From the state of Self-Awareness, you will be able to answer this question for yourself. If you answer it from a Work point of view, you will begin to separate from these Negative Emotions. With repeated Observation, Understanding grows, Separation continues and you CAN make efforts to eliminate this feeling (Negative Emotion) which is responsible for the original set of habitual Negative I's. The Work says that a person can DO the Work. It is through Understanding, from practical experience and the effort to not Identify, that you can become free of this one particular bit of Wrong Work. Understanding is illumination, and lies so Negative Emotions cannot exist in its light. Understanding resolves paradoxes and raises you above the level of opposite I's. However, Understanding must be formed in the right way through the honest action of the Work. This is necessary, of course, because everyone thinks they understand all the time, while they still hold onto Negative Emotions through Justification.

Understanding can happen in a moment or it may be a process that lasts for many years, but it is a process regardless of its time frame. And the process begins with Self-Observation which should lead to inner Separation, which should lead to Non-Identification, which should lead to higher states, higher levels of Consciousness, and development of Being. Try to manage this kind of change in levels, that is, raising one set of Negative I's into the light of Self-Observation to create Understanding, thereby rendering them powerless.

CPSIA information can be obtained at www.ICGtesting.com
Printed in the USA
BVOW08s0121030714

358100BV00013B/187/P